Roger D. Upton

Newmarket & Arabia

€ 10,-

17457 c

Roger D. Upton

Newmarket & Arabia

An Examination of the Descent of Racers and Coursers

1987

Olms Presse

Hildesheim · Zürich · New York

Dem Nachdruck liegt ein Mikrofilm des Exemplares der British Library London zugrunde.

Signatur: 707 e. 10

Nachdruck der Ausgabe London 1873
Printed in Germany
Herstellung: strauss offsetdruck gmbh, 6945 Hirschberg 2
Umschlagentwurf: Prof. Paul König, Hildesheim
ISBN 3 487 08283 7

ARAB HORSES.

NEWMARKET & ARABIA

AN EXAMINATION OF THE DESCENT OF

RACERS AND COURSERS

BY

ROGER D. UPTON

(CAPTAIN LATE 9TH ROYAL LANCERS)

HENRY S. KING & Co.

65 CORNHILL & 12 PATERNOSTER ROW, LONDON

1873

PREFACE.

IN OFFERING the present volume to the public, I will briefly state, the object is to encourage a more general knowledge of and a deeper insight into the history of the horse in this country, more especially that relating to our standard breed called thoroughbred ; to point out errors that have been committed in the breeding of our horse which have prevented, and ever will prevent, his attaining to a complete and satisfactory degree of excellence.

I ask for a patient perusal of its pages, in the hope that many may see the subject in the same light with myself, and the necessity of action in the matter. Long and constant study of the horse and his history, which from early youth has been a labour of love, only increasing with years, added to considerable practical experience gained in many parts of the world, has convinced me of existing faults, and also led me to see the only way in which a true and useful breed of thoroughbred horses can be established.

I more readily put forward the opinions I entertain,

as I have been frequently urged by many, both at home and abroad, to publish in one volume certain essays and reviews on the subject of horses, which have appeared at different times in various magazines and papers.

There have been also frequent demands for the reproduction, in a separate volume, of the 'Successional and Historic Review of the English Racer from 1689 to the Present Time,' to which, it was requested, tables of pedigrees might be added; but I was unwilling that should appear unless accompanied by the history of the Arabian horse, for 'as in geography we can have no just idea of the situation of one country without knowing that of others, so in history, it is in some measure necessary to be acquainted with the whole to comprehend a part.' So, rather than reproduce a number of letters and papers, in which there would be to some extent a want of connection, and necessarily a repetition, I have chosen to write a fresh work giving a history of the Arabian, a knowledge of which is indispensable to a thorough appreciation of the history of the English horse, and in which the whole subject has been enlarged and more fully discussed.

It may perhaps surprise some to find the 'English Uhlan' to be one and the same with the author of the 'Successional and Historic Review of the English Racer,' whose letters in support of Arabian blood appeared about the same time, and although they were not recognised as coming from the same pen it was sufficiently gratifying to find that the views elucidated in the letters of the former were publicly admitted to be confirmed by the latter, and had led, at least in one instance, to a positive indorsement of the opinions urged by the 'English Uhlan.'

For the completion of the First Part, 'The English Horse,' the pedigrees of Herod, Eclipse, and Trumpator have been given at full length, which it, is hoped, may be of great assistance to the reader; these, being traced back to the furthest extent, will enable any one to form a just appreciation of the breeding of the English racer, and at the same time will show conclusively how far short he is of being of pure blood. Trumpator, through horses of mixed and common blood (such as would now be called half-bred), inherited not less than 207 strains of impure blood—this is counting Turks and Barbs as of equally pure blood with Arabians, but which in reality cannot be allowed; therefore the strains of inferior blood are in excess of what is stated. Eclipse inherited at least 86, and Herod a similar number.

The modern racer, being in every instance descended from one or all of the above-named horses, not only inherits these stains, but as often as these horses appear in his pedigree (which they do over and over again) are the original number of stains doubled or quadrupled, as the case may be, and, it must be remembered, faults more readily appear than perfections. Pedigrees of some, if not of all the horses and mares which, although foaled in England, appear to have been entirely of Arabian, Turkish, and Barb blood (these were racers, stallions, and brood mares in the beginning of the last century and the latter end of the preceding one), have also been added, as well as a catalogue of most; and I believe, as nearly as possible, a complete list of the Arabians, so-called Arabians, Barbs, and Turks, which were employed in the formation of the English stud, from the time of King James I. to the end of the last century.

It will be seen the Arabians are in excess of either Barbs or Turks. It would be wrong to encourage the belief that Turks and Barbs were either Arabians or even altogether of unmixed Arab blood; and I think it more than doubtful whether all those horses styled Arabians were really so. Of the Darley Arabian we are quite sure, and what a brilliant example we had of his quality in his son Flying Childers!

It cannot fail to be noticed, there were but few Eastern mares, and those were principally Barbs. With one exception, the royal mares can only be considered of uncertain origin.

The Second Part, 'The History of the Arabian,' may, perhaps, be considered rather long, but it is a subject that might well be enlarged. My only regret is that it should not have been in hands which could have done it full justice. It was necessary to show the antiquity and purity of the race, although the Arabian horse is a living witness, and both outwardly and inwardly speaks for himself. He is one by himself.

I cannot refrain from expressing admiration at the zeal, patience and perseverance, skill and ability, displayed by the framers of the 'General Stud Book,' and the first volume is marvellous.

It only remains for me to thank many friends and authors for their kind assistance, and for the information I have derived from them. I do not mention them by name, knowing it would not be agreeable to some of them; but perhaps it may be interesting to learn that much that has been stated about the Arabian horse—especially of his habitat and oneness—has been fully confirmed by an Arab gentleman of a Nejdean family, who was gratified by the interest I took in Arabian horses, and at the knowledge I had acquired of his country, its tribes and horses.

October, 1872.

ROGER D. UPTON,
Capt. late 9th Royal Lancers.

CONTENTS.

PART 1.

THE ENGLISH HORSE.

CHAPTER I.

CHAPTER II.

CHAPTER III.

PART 2.

THE ORIGIN AND ANTIQUITY OF THE ARABIAN.

PART 3.

CHAPTER I.

CHAPTER II.

PART II

CHAPTER I

[illegible]

CHAPTER II

[illegible]

HORSES:

AN EXAMINATION OF THE DESCENT OF RACERS AND COURSERS.

PART 1.

THE ENGLISH HORSE.

CHAPTER I.

An inquiry as to the breeding of the English racer—Different opinions entertained—The term 'thorough-bred,' in its usual acceptance, with regard to the English horse—Its real signification—Dissertation on the horse in Britain, and a sketch of his history from the earliest period to the reign of Queen Anne—Horses of entirely Eastern blood in England in Queen Anne's time—Highest state of excellence arrived at in Flying Childers—Eastern blood relinquished, and horses and mares of mixed origin again used—The modern racer not thorough-bred, nor even altogether of Eastern blood—Purer at a former period than now.

As purity of blood is deemed necessary for the attainment of any great excellence in the horse, the question whether the English horse, of racing blood, is thorough-bred, is very important.

There are some who maintain that the English horse, as accounted for in the Stud Book, is of entirely Arabian blood, 'the true son of Arabia Deserta, without a drop of English blood in his veins.' If such can be proved to be the case, our horse is entitled to be called thorough-bred.

Others hold the opinion that our horse's excellence is to be attributed to the consummate skill in breeding exhibited in this country, rather than to the procuration of original stock of good description. And there are some who have no knowledge of the history or antecedents of our thorough-bred horse.

What is generally understood by the term 'thorough-bred' is any horse or mare which may have a place in the Stud Book, and can be traced partly (certainly not altogether) up to Arabians, Barbs, Turks, Persian, Egyptian, and other horses of Eastern blood, which, to say the least, is a very vague and incomplete definition or explanation of the term.

Thorough-bred means bred from the *best* blood, completely bred; or, it might be put, completely or entirely bred from the best blood—not merely the best that may be at hand, but the very best procurable—such which has been kept pure, and has not suffered from degeneracy; bred completely from a pure and original race.

The state of the horse in this country at the time immediately preceding the arrival of the Darley Arabian appears to bear some resemblance to that of the inhabitants of England during the Saxon period, before the Conquest. Although nominally Saxon, for a long period Norse blood had been dispersed throughout the land. Norsemen, from Norway and Denmark, the same race, had overrun many parts of England; and at the time of the Conquest the country was ready to receive a further infusion of the same blood from the chivalrous Normans. So was it with the horse. Arabian blood had been introduced from time to time; horses and mares described as Barbs and Turks, more or less of Arabian descent, had been freely used, and a great change had been wrought in the native horse. Then came the Darley Arabian, whose son, Flying Childers, is the best-bred horse to be found in the Stud Book.

Although it may not be of much consequence to speculate upon the type of horse Cæsar found in Britain, it would still be deeply interesting to inquire whether the earliest inhabitants of Northern and Western Europe, the Kimmerians and the Kelts, were possessed of horses; whether the Kumry brought the horse with them from the Bosphorus across the wilds of Europe to the Kimbric Chersonese; whether the horse was brought into Britain by one of the first three immigrations of the Kumry, or by the later ones of the Belgæ, offshoots from the Germans, belonging to the second great tide of population which overran Europe from Asia, and whom we know were possessed of horses in immense numbers. One thing we know: that the horse did not precede man as an inhabitant of these isles, as, when Hu Cadarn, 'the strong or mighty,' led over the first migration of the Kumry, before him there were no inhabitants in Britain, and the country was occupied only by bears, wolves, beavers, and oxen with large protuberances, similar or identical with the denizens of the great Hyrcinian Forest. After Cæsar's time, and during the Roman occupation, it has been suggested, and with much probability, that the British horse would consist of a compound of the native animal and those from Gaul, Italy, Spain, and every province from which the Roman cavalry was supplied. Perhaps the first introduction of Arabian blood took place at this time. Hannibal's cavalry, principally Numidian, had overrun Spain, part of Gaul, and Italy, whose horses were doubtless more or less of Arabian descent. It would also be interesting to learn whether our Saxon forefathers, in their exodus from still further east, when they entered Europe with the second great human wave of population, brought horses with them from the banks of the Araxes; whether, when long settled in Jutland, Sleswig, and Holsatia, previous to their entrance into England under the banner of the White Horse, they still retained those horses, and what effect they had upon the compound breed of Roman Britain.

One thing is certain: during the Saxon period the horses sent by Hugh Capet to Athelstan were highly prized by him, as were also their descendants; and it is more than probable that these owed their excellence to a direct infusion of Arabian blood, as Charlemagne, predecessor to Hugh Capet, had received one or more Arabian horses from his equally celebrated contemporary, the Caliph Haroun el Raschid. These infusions would, of course, be slight.

The next importation came with William the Conqueror, when the Spanish horse was introduced. William's charger [1] was a Spaniard, and several of his barons

[1] He is also described as a Spanish Barb.

seem to have bred from Spanish stallions. But the best horses in Spain were those which had been derived from the cross with the horses of Arabian blood of the Saracens, who had for so long a time held sway in Spain. This was doubtless a more important cross, and would change the character of the breed to some considerable extent, although it must not be thought that the Spanish horse introduced by the Normans much resembled the Arabian, but he had derived certain good qualities. The next opportunity of an introduction of Eastern blood would be in the long period of the Crusades; but this opportunity was not made much of, although the mail-clad champions found out the superiority of the Arabian horse.

The first recorded instance of an Arabian horse in this country was in the reign of Henry I., when Alexander I. of Scotland introduced an Arab horse; and it has been stated (but with no certain records) that an improved breed was derived from this horse.

But King John imported horses of a different stamp, namely, stallions from Flanders, which, good as they may have been for draught, must have done incalculable harm to the progress of the English riding-horse. Then came thirty war-horses from Lombardy, and twelve heavy draught-horses imported by Edward II.; and Edward III. purchased fifty Spanish horses. With these conflicting elements the prosperity of the horse in this country rose and fell.

It would appear, however, that even in the reign of Henry VIII. the state of the English horse was by no means very satisfactory, and that there were almost as great a variety of kinds as in the present day; and which might, indeed, be expected, from the strange admixture. There were the Gentil horse, the palfrey, and the 'grete doble or double trottynge horse,' from among others; the first doubtless bred with more care and more exclusively from the importations from Southern Europe, the last-named showing, no doubt, a large preponderance of the Flemish blood.

The earlier races were contested by horses of all kinds, but gradually a system of training was established, and certain horses selected or bred as racers, improved by the importations from the Levant. King James I. resolved to try the Arab, and bought one for 500*l.* from Mr. Markham. I have no means of ascertaining the antecedents of this horse, and it is very questionable if he were much used as a sire, the then Master of the Horse having taken a great dislike to the little bony horse. Charles I. established races at Newmarket, but during his disturbed reign but little was accomplished, except that it became apparent during the civil war that the Eastern importations had rendered essential service, by the increased activity of the cavalry. Charles II. re-inaugurated the races at Newmarket, and gave plates to be run for, and bought horses and mares of Eastern blood, principally Barbs and Turks, and also mares which were termed royal mares, as were also their descendants, and were of no very certain origin. Some, it has been stated, were purchased in Hungary.

Such is a very brief sketch of our horse up to the

end of the reign of James II. During the reigns of William III. and Queen Anne a fresh impulse was given to racing and the improvement of horses for the Turf. The horses imported during the reign of Charles II. were principally Barbs and Turks; indeed, I expect the Duke of Newcastle having so strong a prejudice against Markham's Arabian was one of the causes why Arabian blood was not more diligently sought for; but in these latter reigns every variety of Eastern blood would appear to have been introduced, and it showed its superiority over the original stock. By this, I take it, is meant the horse as improved by Eastern blood from the time of James I. to William III., not the stock of the country of an earlier date. This is easily accounted for, as at this period there were some horses not of pure Arab blood, but altogether of Eastern extraction, without any admixture of common blood, and these horses showed their superiority over those of mixed origin. Among such were Basto, by the Byerly Turk; Bay Pigot, by Old Careless; Blossom, Careless, Leedes, and Sister to Leedes, and Charming Jenny, also sister to Leedes by the Leedes Arabian; Lord Lonsdale's Counsellor, (Dyer's) Dimple, by the Leedes Arabian; and the two Childers, and Lord Lonsdale's Darley Arabian mare. Those who have expressed the opinion that our horse attained his highest perfection in Flying Childers I believe were perfectly correct.

Strange to say, from the time of the Childers this system of breeding was neglected; and instead of pursuing the plan of carrying on the Eastern blood unmixed, that of breeding from horses and mares of mixed blood, or of putting mares of mixed blood to horses of Eastern blood, was again pursued ; and our present breed of horses traced through the three lines of descent from the Byerly Turk, Darley Arabian, and Godolphin Arabian, or Barb, have all come through horses and mares of mixed blood, being more or less of the old native stock, or from unknown mares. No wonder, in the days of Hobgoblin and Shakespear, although coming immediately after Flying Childers, deterioration was discovered. The fact is, the horse had gone back to the state before the importation of the Leedes and Darley Arabian. Our modern racer has been derived from three branches or lines, and every individual has descended from either Eclipse, Herod, or Trumpator, or a combination of all three, which horses had many flaws in their pedigrees—they were only half-bred.

The very fact that at this period many horses (see table of pedigrees) were bred entirely of Eastern blood, and especially that Arabian blood had been more freely used, is sufficient to account for the superiority shown by such over the horses of a preceding period and also of their own time, which were only of Eastern blood mixed with or engrafted upon the old native stock, and shows that the horse in England had attained at this time to a degree of excellence unknown before in this country ; and taking into consideration how imperfect and inferior the breeding of our horse was immediately after the time of Childers—and which will be more apparent from the pedigrees in the next chapter—it may be safely advanced that such a degree of excellence has not been known since. This may be considered bold language ; but that the racer was purer bred then than at any later period, or even now, cannot be denied.

CHAPTER II.

A successional and historic review of the English race horse, from the year 1689 to the present time.

It is purposed to give a sketch of the English race horse from the year 1689 up to the present time, and to take the three imported horses, known as the Darley Arabian, the Byerly Turk, and the Godolphin Arabian, and trace from them separately the various families that have sprung from them in direct male descent. The other imported horses are not brought in, as they have not handed down their blood in direct male descent, although they did their work by improving the blood of the former running horse of this country; among such are the Helmsley Turk, Place's Turk, Lister's Turk, D'Arcey White and Yellow Turks, Dodsworth, the Belgrade Turk, and perhaps prominently among these importations, Curwen's bay Barb, Sir J. Williams's Turk (or Honeywood's Arabian), Bloody Buttocks, and the Leedes Arabian. Nor has it been attempted to give here a full list of the Eastern horses brought to this country. It is more than likely Markham's Arabian was not used at all, although King James I. gave 500 guineas for him, as the prejudice was very strong against the Arabian, and the Master of the Horse took a dislike to him. Although small, it is quite possible he may have been a horse of excellent blood. The imported horses were used among the mares of the country; a mixture, perhaps, of every kind of horse under the sun, or nearly so. But besides these were others: King Charles II. sent abroad to procure a number of *foreign* horses and mares for breeding; the mares thus imported were called royal mares, as were also many of their produce; these also enter into the composition of our race horse; they were probably partly of Eastern blood. Next it is proposed to show how these various families are represented at the present time at the stud, or by horses which may have lately retired from the Turf, or may be about to leave, and which may be likely to appear as sires. Some horses may be mentioned at greater length, and other matters brought forward to help deductions being drawn, and which, it is hoped, may be rather interesting than tedious. As the eldest, the line from the Byerly Turk shall first come under consideration.

The Byerly Turk's Line.

Captain Byerly's charger, used by him in 1687 in King William's wars in Ireland, does not seem to have been much patronised at the stud, but he was the sire of Sprite, thought to have been nearly as good as Leedes, who was a son of the Leedes Arabian (Leedes was a horse of entirely Eastern blood); but Sprite did not hand down the Byerly Turk's line, and we must look to Jigg, whose dam was by Spanker. Jigg begot Partner from a sister to Mixbury, who was by Curwen's bay Barb.

The latter was a present to Louis XIV. from Muly Ishmael, King of Morocco. Partner was the sire of Tartar, whose dam, Meliora, was by Fox (Fox's sire, Clumsy, was only half-bred, but Fox's dam was a finely-bred mare, *entirely of Eastern blood*, and very similarly bred to the dam of the two Childers). Tartar was foaled 1743, and was the sire of King Herod, commonly called Herod, whose dam, Cypron, notwithstanding certain flaws in her pedigree, was a highly-bred mare, having two direct strains of the Darley Arabian in her veins (her sire, Blaze, was a grandson of the Darley Arabian). Herod had two sons—Woodpecker, foaled in 1773, and Highflyer in 1774—who handed down his blood through two rival families. Woodpecker's dam, Miss Ramsden, was by Cade, a son of the Godolphin Arabian. The dam of Highflyer was Rachel, by Blank, also a son of the Godolphin Arab, from a Bartlet Childers mare.

Although Woodpecker and Highflyer were similarly bred, the former is a particularly well-bred horse, and worthy of special notice. He traces back to the Darley Arabian through a mare who played a very conspicuous part in the English stud—Lord Lonsdale's Darley Arabian mare. Miss Ramsden's dam was by the Lonsdale bay Arabian, her granddam by Bay Bolton, her great granddam the Darley Arabian mare, entirely of Eastern blood. Pursuing the system of going by seniority, the line from Herod through Woodpecker, the elder son, will be first reviewed.

In 1787 Buzzard was accredited to him ; a chestnut like his sire ; his dam, Misfortune, was by Dux, by Matchem, a son of Cade, of the Godolphin Arab line. Buzzard was the sire of three celebrated chestnut horses, to wit, Castrel, Selim, and Rubens, foaled respectively in the years 1801, 1802, and 1805. Their dam, the Alexander mare, has often been styled the most remarkable mare in the Stud Book. Without going quite so far, in all justice it may be said there are few more celebrated; her sire, Alexander, was by Eclipse, from Grecian Princess. The dam of the Alexander mare was by Highflyer. Castrel, the eldest of the three brothers, begot Merlin, foaled in 1815, and Pantaloon, a chestnut with dark spots, in 1824. Pantaloon was the sire of Sleight of Hand, foaled in 1836. The late Sir Tatton Sykes was very partial to the blood, and had very many of his mares in his stud. 1841 was a great year for Pantaloon, as his daughter, Ghuznee, won the Oaks, and his son, Satirist, the Doncaster St. Leger, beating Coronation, the Derby winner, for whom the St. Leger was looked upon as a certainty. In the same year Satirist also astonished the public by carrying off the Gold Vase at Ascot from Lanercost. He was a bay-brown horse; his dam Sarcasm, a brown mare, by Teniers, a son of Rubens, from Banter (Touchstone's dam), by Master Henry.

Ghuznee was a bright bay, and through her dam Languish, also bay, traced back to Herod (the founder of both the Woodpecker and Highflyer lines), through Cain, Paulovitz, Sir Paul, Sir Peter Teazle (commonly called Sir Peter), and Highflyer. She was a very fine and strongly-formed mare, although *only* 15 *hands and half an inch*, and was pronounced by Mr. George Tattersall to be of a shape peculiarly calculated to make a superior brood mare. Pantaloon was the sire of The Libel, foaled in 1842, a brown horse from a Camel mare. He was the sire of the following also:—Elthiron, a very neat horse, foaled in 1846; Windhound, foaled in 1847; Hernandez, in 1848 (winner of the Two Thousand Guineas); Hobbie Noble, in 1849, quite a sensational horse; The Reiver, in 1850; and Miserrima, a brown filly, foaled in 1848. Elthiron, Windhound, Miserrima, Hobbie Noble, and The Reiver, were all from one mare, Lord Westminster's Phryne, by Touchstone. The three former were brown, the two latter bay; their Touchstone dam may have influenced their colour.

But to return to Windhound, in whom we are most concerned, as the reputed and generally accepted sire of Thormanby, winner of the Derby in 1860, now at the stud, with a chance of making himself a name, if he has not already done so. The beautiful and celebrated Alice Hawthorn, whose breeding will be commented upon further on, was the dam of Thormanby.

Presuming Thormanby to be the *bonâ fide* son of Windhound, he must certainly be put down as the best representative of the line at the present day, and the honour of the family would appear to be confided to his keeping.

The blood of the Darley Arabian and of the Godolphin Arab was first introduced into the Turk's line in Herod through the dam of Blaze, the latter the sire of Cypron (Herod's dam). The dam of Blaze, the Confederate filly, was by Confederate, by Conductor, of the

Godolphin Arab's line, but Herod had three strains of the Darley Arabian's blood through the same mare, and two from Cypron, his own dam. Since then fresh strains from both lines have been continually brought into the Byerly Turk's line. Sometimes the blood of one has predominated over the other, and it is very interesting to consider whether the larger admixture of the Darley Arabian blood in some horses may not have given greater stoutness than is seen in others, who had less of that and more of the Godolphin Arab's blood. That such has been the case I trust will become apparent to those who may have the patience to follow me, particularly those interested in the welfare of our horse, and who may not have time, patience, or opportunity to unravel the mazes of the Stud Book.

We must now cast back to the year 1802, and trace the Woodpecker line, through his grandson, Selim, the second son of Buzzard.

Selim, grandson of Woodpecker, foaled in 1802, a chestnut, and own brother to Castrel, was the sire of a brown filly, dam by Cesario, winner of the One Thousand Guineas in 1815; of Medora, winner of the Oaks in 1814; of Azor, winner of the Derby in 1817; of Turcoman, winner of the Two Thousand Guineas in 1827, whose dam, Pope Joan, was by Waxy; and of Turquoise, winner of the Oaks in 1828; of Sultan, foaled in 1816; and Langar in 1817. These last two we shall take for our consideration.

Sultan, a magnificent bay horse with a blaze and four white feet, the off hind-leg white half way to the hock;

his dam was Bacchante, a brown mare, by Williamson's Ditto (a son of Sir Peter, grandson of Herod, from Arethusa, by Dungannon, son of Eclipse). Bacchante's dam was sister to Calomel, by Mercury, son of Eclipse out of Folly, by Marske, great-grandson of the Darley Arabian, tracing back to Herod and the Darley Arabian through many sources. It has been asserted that Sultan bore a strong resemblance to the Darley Arabian—it will be seen he inherited much of his blood; he has been described to me by one who knew him well as a splendid animal, but perhaps hardly deep enough in the chest. Looking at his portrait by Herring which is before me, I should say the deficiency was in appearance only; he seems to have been a very level-made horse, with deep back ribs, which formation always takes off from the appearance of a deep chest. This formation (of deep back ribs) seems to have been general among the racers of an elder period, and is characteristic of Arabian blood. The modern racer is lighter in his ribs, not so round, and less deep in the back ribs, which shows the chest as more deep. He had a fine head, with much of the Arabian character in it, small and finely-formed ears, well pricked. I am not sure whether Sultan ought not to be written down as the best representative of the Woodpecker line, if not of the Herod, but of that opinions can be formed hereafter. His career at the stud was certainly most brilliant. Among others he was the sire of the following horses:—Beiram, Ishmael, Jereed; of Greenmantle, winner of the Oaks, 1829 (her dam Dulcinea, by Cervantes); of Augustus, winner of the Two

Thousand Guineas in 1830 (his dam Augusta, by Woful); of Galata, winner of the One Thousand Guineas and the Oaks in 1832 (whose dam Advance was by Pioneer); of the magnificent Glencoe, winner of the Two Thousand Guineas in 1834 (whose dam, Trampoline, was by Tramp out of Web, by Waxy). Glencoe was the sire of Pocahontas (the dam of Stockwell); of Ibrahim, winner of the Two Thousand Guineas in 1835, whose dam, a Phantom mare, was sister to Cobweb (Bay Middleton's dam); of Achmet (own brother to Bay Middleton), winner of the Two Thousand Guineas in 1837; of Destiny, winner of the One Thousand Guineas in 1836, and of that splendid racehorse, Bay Middleton, winner of the Two Thousand Guineas and the Derby in 1836. Before proceeding further with the Sultan family, I purpose taking up the history of Langar, the other son of Selim, before mentioned, to enable us to review the career of his son Elis, who was contemporary with Bay Middleton, and to some extent his rival. Langar, a chestnut horse, foaled in 1817, from a Walton mare (whose dam, Young Giantess, was by Diomed, out of Giantess, by Matchem, son of Cade, son of Godolphin Arab or Barb), was the sire of Elis and Epirus, both chestnuts, and own brothers; their dam was Olympia, by Sir Oliver. Elis, foaled in 1833, had a white face, and both hind legs white, was the winner of the St. Leger in 1836, beating among others the celebrated Beeswing. Epirus, foaled in 1834, was the sire of Pyrrhus the First, a bright chestnut, with two hind feet white, and a white reach down his face; his dam was Fortress, by Defence; he won the Derby in 1846, beating Sir Tatton Sykes by a neck. Having such stout blood as Defence's in his veins from his dam, it was expected he would have been a success at the stud—that, as is often the case with expectations, was not realised (the blood on his dam's side was too good to allow of his being a successful sire)—however, he was the sire of the celebrated Virago, winner of the One Thousand Guineas in 1854. But to return to Bay Middleton, his dam Cobweb (herself winner of the One Thousand Guineas, 1824) was by Phantom out of Filagree, by Soothsayer out of Web, by Waxy, &c. He was a bay colt, but in after years more nearly brown than bay, and mottled on his quarters; standing nearly 16 hands and a half, without white, except on three of his coronets. Although not what could be called a symmetrically made horse, yet he was a splendid animal, and full of character. He ran first without a name, and in the Newmarket Craven Meeting won the Riddlesworth Stakes of 200 sovs. each, beating, among others, his half sister, Destiny, the winner of the One Thousand Guineas. He won as he liked. He had been *considered* a bad tempered horse up to this time, but after winning his race he was changed into a high-couraged one. For the Two Thousand Guineas he met Elis and five others; the Cobweb colt beat Elis on the post by a neck; 'the others were beaten off an immense distance by the extraordinary severity of the pace;' he was then named Bay Middleton. Elis was not in the Derby, 1836, which was won by Bay Middleton by two lengths, with such horses as Gladiator, Venison, and Slane, respectively second, third, and fourth to him. Bay Middleton was not in the St. Leger, which was won by Elis very easily by two lengths. In the same year Bay Middleton and Elis met again in the Newmarket First October Meeting, for the Grand Duke St. Michael Stakes; twenty-one horses were frightened out of the field by their appearance; the race was won by the former by a length. Mr. George Tattersall has thus described it: 'After all, it was a falsely run race, the pace being poor, and each on the lurching order till they passed the Bushes, where Bay Middleton went up; at the top of the hill he was leading, and in going down it his wonderful stride enabled him to show his tail to his gallant opponent. "Honest John" (the rider of Elis) tried what whipping would do, but it was "no go," and the winner of the St. Leger was beaten in pace, stride, and stoutness, by the winner of the Derby.' Here, I think, is a case in point: The greater number of crosses of the Darley Arabian blood in Bay Middleton and his sire Sultan than in Elis and his sire Langar—although Sultan and Langar were half-brothers, both being sons of Selim—will account for Bay Middleton being stouter than Elis. His career was brilliant, but short. A foreleg already looking suspicious prevented his training on, and he retired to the stud in 1838. As a sire he cannot be said to have equalled Sultan. He was the sire of Ellen Middleton, the dam of Wild Dayrell (winner of the Derby, 1855), of Cowl (1842), of The Flying Dutchman (winner of the Derby and St. Leger in 1849), of Aphrodite (winner of the One Thousand Guineas, 1851), of Andover (winner of the Derby in 1854), whose dam was a Defence mare, of Hermit (winner of the Two Thousand Guineas, 1854), from Jenny Lind, by Touchstone.

Andover was a very nice horse, but The Flying Dutchman was the most distinguished of Bay Middleton's sons, and won all his two-year-old engagements without having been fairly extended—the Derby and St. Leger, as before said, and the Emperor's Plate at Ascot. The only time he was beaten was for the Doncaster Cup, by Voltigeur, in 1850, when perhaps he was not thoroughly prepared. Upon his defeat a match of 1,000*l.* a side was made between him and Voltigeur, by the Earls of Eglinton and Zetland, the former giving the latter the choice of ground. It was over two miles of ground, and run at York, 13th May, 1851, the Dutchman defeating Voltigeur by a length. The time was accurately taken—3 minutes 55 seconds. He was a fine-looking horse, dark brown, without white, with springy action, which he generally transmitted to his stock, and inherited from his dam, Barbelle, by Sandbeck, her dam Darioletta, by Amadis. He might be distinguished among a crowd of horses by his grand appearance, and was remarkable for the size of his arms, as was also his sire, Bay Middleton, and this point is also transmitted, as a rule, to his stock. He was the sire of Ellington (winner of the Derby in 1856), of Gildermire, who ran a dead heat for the Oaks of 1858, and of Brown Duchess (winner of the Oaks, 1861). Brown Duchess ran a dead heat with Kettledrum for the Doncaster Cup, but the latter walked over for it afterwards. His son Ellington has not achieved any great stud success, and there is no worthy representative of Bay Middleton and Sultan. The Bay Middleton stock have been pronounced as invariably blood-like in their appearance. I do not hold with this. Many of them had a certain elegance about them, and some were grand-looking, with fine points; but to be blood-like a horse ought to have the symmetry and beauty approaching to the Arabian, from which source the blood was derived, and the term blood-like had its origin. As an example of the Bay Middleton family, I think Himalaya, in Her Majesty's stud, would convey a very just idea, presenting all the grand points, with some of the deficiencies.

We must now consider Rubens, the third son of Buzzard, a chestnut, foaled in 1805, and own brother to Castrel and Selim, as stated before. He is more distinguished for his daughters. He was the sire of Landscape, winner of the Oaks, 1816; of Pastille, winner of the Two Thousand Guineas and the Oaks, 1822 (Pastille's dam was Parasol, by Pot8os, son of Eclipse); and of Whizgig, winner of the One Thousand Guineas the same year. The Two Thousand Guineas, the One Thousand Guineas, and the Oaks having been won by two of his fillies in one year, was certainly a feather in the cap of Rubens. Whizgig was also the dam of Oxygen, winner of the Oaks in 1831. Rubens was also the sire of the dam of Lord Berner's Phosphorus (winner of the Derby, 1837) and of May Day, own sister of

Phosphorus, winner of the One Thousand Guineas, 1834; of Defiance, the dam of Defence; and of Ruby, the dam of Coronation (winner of the Derby, 1841); and of Sir Joshua, foaled in 1812, who defeated Filho da Puta in a match at Newmarket. Sir Joshua's dam was own sister to Filho da Puta's sire. Sir Joshua: a chestnut horse, about fifteen hands, by Rubens out of a Sir Peter mare (sister to Haphazard). Filho da Puta, a bay horse, also foaled in 1812, sixteen hands or over, was by Haphazard (son of Sir Peter and Miss Hervey, by Eclipse); his dam, Mrs. Barnet, by Waxy out of a Woodpecker mare. There is great similarity in the breeding of these two horses, and the strains of Darley Arabian blood in each of them very evenly balanced. This brings us to the end of the Woodpecker branch of the Herod line, great-great-grandson of the Byerly Turk; but before we leave this portion of our subject I wish to allude in a few words to Merlin, a son of Castrel, a chestnut horse, foaled in 1801. He was the sire of Lamplighter, who, in his turn, was the sire of Phosphorus, winner of the Derby in 1837, and of May Day, winner of the One Thousand Guineas in 1834.

Having made this *amende* to Castrel I will only say that I think Sultan must be considered the chief of his family, and his son, Bay Middleton, and his grandson, The Flying Dutchman, the most distinguished racers.

It was stated that King Herod, great-great-grandson of the Byerly Turk, had two sons, Woodpecker and Highflyer, through whom the blood of the Byerly Turk has been handed down in the male line to the present time ; but as King Herod, or, as we shall call him, Herod, was not particularly described, before proceeding to trace the Highflyer branch a slight sketch of this fine horse shall be given. He was a bay horse without white, saving a very small star, standing about 15 hands 3 inches high, of substance, length, and power, foaled in 1758, with a level back and high quarter, and deep in the back ribs. He ran five times for 1,000 guineas each race, and won three out of the five, and won several matches of 500 guineas. He usually, if not invariably, ran over a course of four miles at Newmarket, Ascot, and York ; stoutness and ability to carry weight were his characteristics. His dam, Cypron, was by Blaze, a son of Flying Childers, son of the Darley Arabian ; Cypron's dam Selima, by Bethell's Arabian, from a mare by Graham's Champion, who was by Harpur's Arabian from a mare by the Darley Arabian. Looking at his dam's pedigree, we may well believe him to have been a stout, game horse ; and there are good grounds for believing that the assertion made—viz., that his great-great-grandson, Sultan, bore a strong resemblance to the Darley Arabian—was a correct one.

The list of Herod mares is an extensive one. His daughter Bridget won the first Oaks, in 1779 ; and his daughter Faith won the Oaks in 1781. In 1783 his son Phœnomenon won the St. Leger, and in the same year his daughter Maid of the Oaks won the Oaks. The first Derby (1780) was won by Diomed, grandson of Herod. Tuberose was another of his daughters.

Unlike Woodpecker, Highflyer from Rachel, by Blank,

was bay, like his sire Herod. He never paid forfeit, and was never beaten. It is noteworthy that most of the descendants of Woodpecker were chestnuts, and those of Highflyer for the most part bay. Sultan was bay; but then his dam came from the Highflyer family, and bays and browns were chiefly carried on through his son Bay Middleton. Highflyer also left behind him a goodly roll of mares. His sons Noble and Sir Peter Teazle won the Derby in the years 1786 and 1787; and in 1789 his son Skyscraper won the Derby. In 1792 Vialante, a filly of his, won the Oaks, and his daughters Omphale and Cowslip the St. Leger in 1784 and 1785; his son Spadille in 1787, and his daughter Young Flora, own sister to Spadille, in 1788.

This must suffice for Highflyer, and we select his son, Sir Peter, who hands down his family, for consideration.

Sir Peter Teazle, a brown horse, foaled in 1784, his dam Papillon, was by Snap; Snap by Snip, Snip by Flying Childers. Here we get another infusion of Darley Arabian blood. Besides being the sire of Sir Harry and Archduke, winners of the Derby in 1798 and 1799; of Ditto, who won the Derby in 1803, and who was the sire of Sultan's dam; of Paris, winner of the Derby, 1806, his daughters Hermione and Parasote won the Oaks in 1794 and 1796; and Ambrosio, Fyldener, Paulina, and Petronius were his St. Leger winners in 1796, 1806, 1807, and 1808. He was also the sire of Haphazard, foaled in 1797; of Walton, foaled in 1799; of Sir Oliver, 1800; of Sir Paul, foaled in 1802. Sir Oliver, whose dam was by Diomed, was the sire of

Olympia, the dam of Elis and Epirus. Haphazard, Walton, and Sir Paul have brought down the Sir Peter blood in male descent, and these we shall consider in succession. Haphazard's dam was Miss Hervey, by Eclipse, and he was the sire of Filho da Puta, foaled in 1812. The latter won the St. Leger in 1815; but he was beaten by Sir Joshua, by Rubens, in their celebrated match, run at Newmarket, by a head. He was the first foal of Mrs. Barnet, by Waxy, and was a magnificent horse. Sir Joshua, a chestnut, was a small horse; his dam was own sister to Haphazard, by Sir Peter out of Mrs. Hervey. Filho da Puta was the sire of Birmingham, who won the St. Leger in 1830, and of Colwick, foaled in 1828, whose dam, Stella, was by Sir Oliver. Colwick was a bay horse, and sire of Attila, winner of the Derby in 1842. Attila's dam, Progress, was by Langar. He was a small-sized but a strong-made horse; he had splendid action, and a very light step. Few handsomer or truer-made horses, it has been said, have appeared on the Turf. But it was maintained by some that he was wanting in 'heart.' There is nothing more worthy of notice in this branch of the Sir Peter line; but it may be mentioned that Antar and Reginald, sons of Haphazard, won the Two Thousand Guineas, and his daughter Rowena the One Thousand Guineas.

As a sire Walton must be considered the most distinguished of Sir Peter's sons. He was a bay horse, foaled in 1799, and own brother to Ditto. His dam, Arethusa, by Dungannon, got another strain of the Darley Arabian through her granddam, Virago, by Snap, grandson of Flying Childers. Dungannon was by Eclipse, from Aspasia, by Herod. His son Phantom won the Derby in 1811; and St. Patrick, another son, the Leger in 1820. Phantom (foaled in 1808) was a bay horse; his dam was Julia (sister to Eleanor), got by Whiskey out of Sorcerer's dam, by Diomed, who was a grandson of Herod. Whiskey was by Saltram, from Calash, by Herod. Saltram was by Eclipse, from Virago, by Snap, grandson of Flying Childers. Phantom was the sire of Cedric and Middleton (winners of the Derby in 1824 and 1825), but he is more renowned as the sire of Cobweb (winner of the Oaks in 1824), she being the dam of Bay Middleton. It is quite worthy of note that Walton's own brother, Ditto (whose dam came from the Darley Arabian's line), was the sire of Sultan's dam, Bacchante, and that Walton's son Phantom (whose dam also came from the Darley Arabian's family) was the sire of Cobweb, Bay Middleton's dam, which horse was the son of Sultan. Cobweb was a bay mare; her dam was Filagree, by Soothsayer, from Web, by Waxy (more Darley Arabian blood, but also with an infusion of the Godolphins). However, we must now proceed to look at Partisan, the son of Walton, who handed down the line to the present time. He was a bay horse, foaled in 1811; his dam, Parasol, was by Pot8os (son of Eclipse, great-grandson of Bartlet Childers, son of the Darley Arabian), her dam Prunella, by Highflyer (son of Herod), whose dam was by Blaze (son of Flying Childers, son of the Darley Arabian), from Promise, by Snap (grandson of Flying Childers). I will merely mention that his son Mameluke, whose dam was by Stamford (another son of Sir Peter's), and from an Eclipse mare, was the winner of the Derby in 1827, and that his son Glaucus, whose dam was by Selim, was the sire of Refraction, who won the Oaks in 1845. They were all bay. Glaucus missed the Derby and St. Leger, but defeated Rockingham, the St. Leger winner, the next year (1834) for the Gold Cup at Ascot, about two miles and a half. I will return to Partisan, who handed down the Sir Peter line through two of his sons, Gladiator and Venison, both foaled in 1833. They were of kin to Bay Middleton, and finished second and third to him for the Derby, 1836. Cyprian, his daughter, won the Oaks in the same year; Zeal the One Thousand Guineas in 1821; and his son Patron the Two Thousand Guineas in 1829.

Gladiator, a chestnut, and Venison, bay, were both good-looking horses, with good blood-like heads and fine eyes, which points are to be noticed as a rule in their descendants.

Gladiator went to France, and has done that country very great service; and his daughter, Miss Gladiator, was the dam of Gladiateur.

Pauline, the dam of Gladiator, was by Moses, the winner of the Derby in 1822. Whether Moses was the son of Seymour or of Whalebone I will not pretend to say, but he is generally traced to Whalebone. Be this as it may, Moses's dam was by Gohanna, a grandson of Eclipse, her dam Grey Skin, by Woodpecker out of Silver's dam by Herod; and Gohanna's dam was by Herod. Gladiator was thought to have been of a delicate constitution, but he got good sons and daughters in France. He was the sire of Sweetmeat, foaled in 1842.

Sweetmeat was a very neat horse, a dark brown in colour, like his dam ; and among other winning horses was the sire of Mincemeat and Mincepie, winners of the Oaks in 1854 and 1856; of Macaroni, winner of the Two Thousand Guineas and Derby in 1863; and of Carnival. Sweetmeat's dam was Lollypop, got by Starch or Voltaire; her dam Belinda, by Blacklock. Starch was by Waxy Pope by Waxy ; his dam, Miss Stavely, was by Shuttle, by Young Marske, out of Vauxhall Snap mare.

Macaroni, a brown horse, foaled in 1860, is now at the stud. His performances are fresh in our recollection ; and his stock, which have frequently been placed first by the judge, are growing up before our eyes, and we can form our own opinions. It would be premature to say if he or some other son of Sweetmeat is to hand down the Gladiator branch, which, although not likely to be lost in France, if it had not been for Sweetmeat, would have been a dead letter in this country.

Parmesan, a brown horse, by Sweetmeat, from a well-bred mare, Gruyere, by Verulam, from Jennala, by Touchstone, from Emma, by Whisker, was a very neat horse, but he would be called small. He won the Metropolitan Stakes in 1861, however. As the best public performer Macaroni must be considered for the present, at all events, as the representative of the Gladiator blood in this country. Queen Mary, by Gladiator, out of a mare by Plenipo, out of Myrrha, by Whalebone, is celebrated as being the dam of Blink Bonny, also the dam of Haricot, the dam of Caller Ou.

Venison was a bay horse with a white reach and both hind fetlocks white. He was a very honest, game horse, and although he had not the speed of Bay Middleton he picked up a good many things for his owner between Epsom and Doncaster, and always travelled on foot. He defeated Mündig, the winner of the Derby, 1835, for the King's Plate at Doncaster (four miles), winning in a canter by three or four lengths. Venison's dam, Fawn, had the reputation of being a great jade, and was by Smolensko; her dam, Jerboa, was by Gohanna (grandson of Eclipse) out of Camilla, by Trentham. He was the sire of many winners of more or less note. His son, The Ugly Buck, won the Two Thousand Guineas in 1844. Clementina, his daughter, won the One Thousand Guineas in 1847, and his daughter, Miami, the Oaks the same year. Then there were Red Deer and Red Hart, own brothers, and the handsome Vatican and Cruiser, who was tamed by Rarey, Fallow Buck, Filius, and many others, among which was Chamois, the winner of the first Metropolitan Stakes at Epsom. Venison was the sire of Alarm, foaled in 1842, whose dam, Southdown, was by Defence, a grandson of Waxy. Alarm, a bay horse with a blaze, won the Cambridgeshire in 1845, and the Emperor's Plate at Ascot, 1846. I am afraid as a stud horse, as in the case of Pyrrhus the First, those who expected much were doomed to disappointment, and for similar reasons, although his blood, through his daughters, must be useful. It must not be forgotten that he was the sire of that fine mare, Torment, the dam of Tormentor, winner of the Oaks, 1866. He was a good-looking horse, but we pass on to Kingston (foaled in 1849). His dam, Queen Anne, was by Slane; her dam, Garcia, by Octavian, from a mare by Shuttle, who was by Young Marske from the Vauxhall Snap mare, a piece of breeding very similar to that seen in Sweetmeat's pedigree. He was a very handsome horse, and although he did not win the Derby was a good racer, and pulled off many races; his son, Caractacus, won the Derby in 1862, and his daughter, Queen Bertha, the Oaks in 1863. He was also the sire of Ely, and of numerous mares, many of which were in Mr. Blenkiron's stud.

Caractacus, foaled in 1859, a bay horse, with a blaze, and near hind leg grey, was a good-looking horse; his dam, Defenceless, by Defence; her dam by Cain. Here we have a similarly bred horse to Alarm, and I should say like him in appearance, but very docile and good-tempered. He had beautiful action, and I never saw a better mover on any racecourse—he showed his *gameness* when he ran for the Metropolitan. The Derby of 1862 must be still fresh in the memory of most. Caractacus proved himself to be a racehorse, and although many people thought it a mistake, my own opinion has always been that he won *very* easily, and might have done so by lengths. Although Caractacus possessed certain characteristics of his sire Kingston, and his grandsire Venison, in shape and formation I should say he bore more resemblance to his maternal grandsire, Defence.

Ely, a bay horse, with a few silver hairs, marks which

are to be seen in most, if not all, of the Venisons, fully kept up the renown of the family for gameness. Although he failed to carry off the great prizes of his year, he met with frequent triumphs; he is now at the stud.

King John, by Kingston, from Dinah by Clarion, her dam Rebekah, by Sir Hercules, has many admirers, and it is expected by some that he will be the horse of the family, if not the one of the period. There is still plenty of time for any one of them to make himself a stud name, but neither Caractacus nor Ely appear to have been patronised to the extent their performances might justly warrant. I look upon mares of this family as very valuable, as will also be fillies from the above-named young sires. Ferina, by Venison, foaled in 1844, was the dam of Pretender, the winner of the Derby in 1869.

Sir Paul, the last of the sons of Sir Peter which we have to consider, foaled in 1802, was a bay horse, and own brother to Paulina, winner of the St. Leger; his dam, Pewet, was by Tandem. He was the sire of Paulowitz, a brown horse, foaled in 1813; his dam, Evelina, was by Highflyer, also the dam of Cervantes, by Don Quixote. He was the sire of Archibald, who won the Two Thousand Guineas in 1832; and of Cain, a bay horse foaled in 1822, whose dam was by Paynator. Cain was the sire of Ion, a brown horse, foaled 1835; his dam, Margaret, by Edmund (a son of Orville), from Medora, by Selim. Ion showed in good form as a two-year-old; he ran second to Amato for the Derby in 1838, and was second also for the St. Leger, won by Don John. In a fortunate moment he was selected as the only horse *good enough* for Ellen Middleton, and became the sire of Wild Dayrell, or it is likely nothing more might have been heard of him.

Wild Dayrell, a brown horse, foaled in 1852 (his dam, Ellen Middleton, by Bay Middleton from Myrrha, by Malek), winner of the Derby in 1855, was the sire of Hurricane, winner of the One Thousand Guineas in 1862; but his stud fame is owing principally to his having been the sire of Buccaneer, from a Little Red Rover mare, the dam of Cruiser. Buccaneer is lost to this country; he was foaled in 1857. He has made himself a name through his daughters Formosa and Brigantine. With this exception, I know of no other worthy scion of the line from Sir Peter.

We have now come to the end of the Byerly Turk's line, having traced it through several branches to the present day; and we find the following to be the principal representatives:—Buccaneer abroad; Macaroni, Parmesan, and Carnival; Caractacus, Ely, and King John; Ellington, Dollar, and Thormanby.

Certain memoranda have been mentioned from time to time to arrest the attention of the reader, and to serve as data for him to form his own opinions and come to his own conclusions. The similarity of breeding between Woodpecker and Highflyer was noticed with a special reference to some strains of blood in Woodpecker's pedigree. As a rule the descendants from Herod, through Highflyer and Sir Peter, have been distinguished more for stoutness; those generally from Woodpecker, although with some notable exceptions, rather for great speed; one line generally being distinguished by bays, the other by chestnuts, and both of them being celebrated for the excellences of their mares. My own ideas, derived from studying the pedigrees of the various horses of this line, I am tempted to give, not that I would wish to thrust them upon others, but to be taken for what they may be worth, and also as a reply to any *cui bono*, which may be asked, for all these particulars about horses dead and gone, and many quite forgotten.

First, I must state my conviction is this: The real worth of the family is owing to the blood of the Darley Arabian, first brought into the line in Herod, and it is owing to the frequent and very strong infusions of that blood which have taken place that the line has been so widely spread and so long handed down, and at times had such splendid representatives. I cannot offer, of course, actual proofs, but there are not wanting, to my mind, certain indications, kind of sign posts to the traveller through the mazes of breeding, of which I have availed myself, and which may not have been noticed by many. Partner, the paternal grandsire of Herod, was a bright chestnut; Herod a bay horse. He inherited much of the Darley Arabian blood through his dam Cypron, who was bay. Her sire, Blaze, was bay, as was his sire, Flying Childers, as also was his sire, the Darley Arabian, and ability to run long distances was his *forte*. I think it will be observed by those who may have the patience to read these papers that as a rule when the Darley Arabian blood has been more prominent, and especially when derived from Flying Childers and his sons, there have been more bays ; and the line through Sir Peter evidently containing a stronger infusion of the Darley Arabian blood than those generally through Woodpecker has not only handed down bay horses, but they have been more celebrated for their stoutness and gameness. Sultan, of the Woodpecker line, said to be like the Darley Arabian in figure and appearance, was bay, and he had derived advantage of more Darley Arabian blood through his dam, by Williamson's Ditto, and Sir Peter. Not only was the colour more confirmed in his son, Bay Middleton, but stoutness as well, and through his dam, Cobweb, he had still further infusions of the Darley Arabian blood. It must not be supposed that it is argued the increased stoutness was derived from the change of colour from chestnut to bay, but it is a tolerably fair and conclusive inference that as the bay colour came in and was perpetuated or confirmed by the infusion of the Darley Arabian blood, the increased stoutness and gameness is also to be attributed to the same source, the one being the sign, the other the result. It is true that Highflyer's dam, like Woodpecker's, was from another family, namely, the Godolphin Arabian ; but in the Woodpecker line it was carried on still in Buzzard, whose dam was by a horse of that family ; but in the case of Highflyer it was not so, as his son's (Sir Peter) dam was by Snap, son of Snip, grandson of the Darley Arabian, who seems to have snapped and snipped off some of that blood brought in by Highflyer's dam. I could proceed with this or a similar train of reasoning, but I do not wish to be tedious, or to take up too much space, and I will only add, in conclusion, that I think the blood of this line is more valuable through the mares than through the horses. I do not mean to say that individual great horses may not appear as they have before, but that as the best blood is on the female side, and was originally derived from the female side, the horses may not be always capable of handing down their own individual excellences. On the other hand, the mares having so much of the Darley Arabian blood in their veins put to his male descendants may be most valuable.

One great feature in this line is that it has been *bred up* to excellence. Herod was a great landmark, if the expression may be allowed; he may almost be said to have been a grand starting point, for in him the nature of the *Eastern* blood handed down to him was raised and vivified by a strong infusion of true Arabian blood; thus the character of the breed was materially changed. Whether it reached its zenith in him or in his great-great-grandson, Sultan, I will not pretend to say, for although I think the excellence was abated for two generations, it was revived in the third, and more so in the fourth, which was in Sultan, but I think the greatest benefit that will be derived from this line at the present time and in future will be from its daughters and the daughters which may come from the young sires now at the stud.

The Darley Arabian Line.

The Darley Arabian was a bay horse who possessed, so it has been stated, every point that could be desired in a Turf horse.

He was a Koheilan-Ras-el-Fedawi. The Kaheilan is one of the principal breeds of pure bred Arabians; the adjunct Ras-el-Fedawi specifies one of the numerous varieties of this family. Mr. Darley, who was consul at Aleppo, obtained this horse, I believe, during one of the annual visits of the great Anezah of Nejed, which tribe goes annually from thence to within a few miles of Aleppo in the spring, and returns to Nejed in the autumn or winter. He had a white snip down his face; his two hind feet and off fore foot were white.

The Stud Book informs us that he covered very few mares except Mr. Darley's, who had very few well-bred ones.

He was the sire of Childers, commonly called Flying Childers, Almanzor, and his own brother, Cupid, Brisk, Aleppo, and some few others.

Bartlet's Childers is generally supposed to have been own brother to Flying Childers, and the Darley Arabian line is traced from him through Eclipse, supposed to be great-grandson of Bartlet's Childers, the blood of Flying Childers being more generally represented in the line of the Byerly Turk. It would have been, I think, more satisfactory had Flying Childers handed down the line in direct male descent; but the usually admitted succession is as follows:—Bartlet's Childers, Squirt, Marske,

Eclipse. Spiletta, the dam of Eclipse, was also covered by Shakespear, and there are some who think he was the sire of Eclipse; if they be right, the line of succession would be—Flying Childers, Aleppo, Hobgoblin, Shakespear, Eclipse; but as I have no convincing evidence to bring forward in support of Shakespear having been the sire of Eclipse, I must content myself with only alluding to the doubt that has arisen, and pursue for consideration the line from Bartlet's Childers.

Unfortunately, a doubt has been expressed about Bartlet's Childers. The Stud Book says he was for several years called Young Childers, it being generally supposed that he was own brother to the Devonshire Childers (Flying Childers), though some insisted that Betty Leedes never produced any other foal than Flying Childers, except one that was choked when very young by eating chaff. Mr. Cheney says, 'he has heard the contrary from so many gentlemen of worth and honour, that he cannot but be of opinion that he was own brother to him.' He was never trained, and was the sire of Squirt, Œdipus, and the Little Hartley mare, &c.

Flying Childers was a bay horse, about 15 hands high, with a blaze and four white feet. He is usually represented in woodcuts and engravings as a very well-formed horse, but with a prominent and bony head between the eyes and for some way down the face. I have seen a large oil painting which represents him with a very fine head of the Arabian type, with a wide forehead, and flat between the eyes, tapering and slightly dished before coming to the muzzle, and with a fine full eye, with a straight back and high quarters, long shoulders, not very deep in chest, but deep in the back ribs, so that the underneath line carried from the elbow along the belly was very nearly straight, a similar formation and appearance to those described in Sultan's sketch. There is good reason for believing this representation to be more correct than that shown by the prints, which represent him with that formation of head which tells of base blood, when it is remembered that Flying Childers was a horse altogether of *Eastern* blood, and very nearly Arabian. His sons Blaze and Snip infused his blood very largely into the line of the Byerly Turk. Supposing Bartlet's Childers to have been his own brother, we shall find the line for some time breeding down from a more excellent state to one of less purity, unlike the Turk's line upwards, from an inferior to a better. The Turk's line was improved by frequent infusions of Arabian blood. In the Darley Arabian's line the blood was departed from at once with giant strides.

Squirt, a chestnut horse, foaled in 1732, by Bartlet's Childers, was from a Snake mare without any certain Arabian blood in her veins, and Snake cannot be considered as more than half bred, being by the Lister Turk, his dam by Hautboy, but who was her dam? besides, Hautboy was by a Turk out of a Royal mare, which may have been of any breed.

Marske, by Squirt, foaled in 1750, was a brown horse.

His dam was got by *Mr. Hutton's* Blacklegs (not the Blacklegs by Flying Childers, but by a bay Turk). Her dam was by Bay Bolton out of a mare, by Fox Cub. He got a little more Arabian blood here, as the dam of Fox Cub was by the Leedes Arabian, but there is no other Arab strain, and the pedigree is full of flaws. In these two horses we have no direct return to Arab blood except in the case of the slight infusion of the Leedes Arabian just mentioned, but no instance of breeding back to the Darley Arabian through daughters of Flying Childers, or through mares by any of his sons; and it can be well imagined that these two horses, Squirt and Marske, who had common blood in their veins, could not compare with Flying Childers, who was very nearly of pure Arabian blood.

We have now come down to Eclipse, a chestnut horse, quite sixteen hands, if not more, foaled in 1764. His dam Spiletta, foaled in 1749, was by Regulus, her dam Mother Western, by Smith's son of Snake from a mare by Old Montague, from a mare by Hautboy from a mare by Brimmer—no direct Arab blood, but Eastern mixed with common blood, and many flaws in the pedigree. But Regulus was the son of the Godolphin Arab or Barb, and this is the first time his blood was brought into the line from the Darley Arabian. The Godolphin will be spoken of hereafter, when we come to consider the line he established in direct male descent. The dam of Regulus was Grey Robinson, by the Bald Galloway. She was of the usual mixture of

Eastern and common blood, but without any direct Arabian strain.

Now it must be mentioned how the Godolphin was first brought forward. The Bald Galloway, the sire of the dam of Regulus, was also the sire of Roxana. Hobgoblin, son of Aleppo, son of Flying Childers, was to have been her mate; but he refusing to cover her she was handed over to the Godolphin, who was used as a teaser. This was in 1731. The produce was Lath, 1732. Seven years later Regulus was born to the Godolphin, and his daughter Spiletta was covered by both Marske (grandson of Bartlet's Childers) and by Shakespear (son of Hobgoblin), this latter horse being a grandson of Flying Childers; hence the doubt as to which was the sire of Eclipse. Shakespear was a chestnut horse, foaled in 1745; his dam, the Little Hartley mare, was by Bartlet's Childers from Flying Whig, by Williams's Woodstock Arabian.

But to return to Eclipse, so named from the great eclipse of the sun in 1764, the year of his birth. No horse that he met was able to extend him. He is said to have run the course at York in eight minutes. This was the only race in which it is supposed he was timed. The only contemporary who was thought to have any pretensions to rival Eclipse was Goldfinder, foaled the same year (1764). He has been described as a beautiful and long-reached brown horse, and, like Eclipse, was never beaten. Accident prevented the two meeting, which is to be regretted. Goldfinder was by Snap, grandson of Flying Childers. Though he, too, was not without flaws in his pedigree, I question if he were not a better bred horse than the great Eclipse. Before leaving Eclipse it is well to state that, as a rule, 'the produce of Eclipse ran too generally and exclusively to speed, and that in stoutness and continuance they were greatly surpassed by their competitors on the course, the stock of King Herod and Goldfinder.' [1]

Eclipse was the sire of three Derby winners: Young Eclipse, in 1781, Saltram, in 1783, and Serjeant, in 1784; of one winner of the Oaks, Annette, in 1787; but no St. Leger winner is accredited to him. His blood was handed down in male descent, principally through Pot8os, King Fergus, Joe Andrews, and Mercury.

First was Pot8os, a chestnut horse, foaled in 1773; his dam Sportmistress was by Warren's Sportsman, who was by Cade, a son of the Godolphin Arabian, from Silvertail, by Whitenose, who was by the Hall Arabian, and through Silvertail inherited one other strain of the Darley Arabian blood. Pot8os was the sire of three Derby winners, one Oaks winner, and one winner of the St. Leger—namely, Waxy, Champion, winner of the Derby and St. Leger, and Tyrant, and Nightshade, winner of the Oaks, 1788.

Waxy was a bay horse, foaled in 1790, his dam Maria, by Herod, her dam Lisette, by Snap out of Miss Windsor, by the Godolphin Arab. He has been called, and I think not inaptly, the ace of trumps of the Stud Book.

[1] Remarks on Eclipse's produce in Scott's 'Sportsman's Repository.'

In him the Darley Arabian blood was returned to by several strong infusions, as Maria had two strains of his blood, and one of these by Blaze, son of Flying Childers, and her dam Lisette, had two, one of them by Snap (her sire), who was a grandson of Flying Childers, so that Waxy had five fresh infusions through his dam, and two of them through Flying Childers.

Waxy was the sire of Pope, Whalebone, Blucher, and Whisker (all Derby winners), and of Music, Minuet, and Corinne (winners of the Oaks). These were all bays except Corinne and Whalebone, who were brown.

Whalebone and Whisker were own brothers, Music and Minuet own sisters. Pope was foaled in 1806, his dam Prunella, by Highflyer, from Promise, by Snap. His career was principally in Ireland. Whalebone, foaled in 1807, was the most distinguished of Waxy's sons. His dam Penelope was by Trumpator, from Prunella, by Highflyer, from Promise, by Snap. He was the sire of Lapdog and Spaniel (both Derby winners), both bay, and of Caroline (winner of the Oaks), also a bay, and the line was handed down by three of his sons, Camel, Defence, and Sir Hercules. His son Waverly was the sire of The Saddler, and a reputed sire of Don John (winner of the St. Leger in 1838), as Whalebone was of Moses (the winner of the Derby in 1822).

Three distinguished branches have sprung from these three horses, which we must consider in the order they stand. First, Camel, a brown horse with a blaze and hind feet white, was from a Selim mare, whose dam was Maiden, by Sir Peter. He was the sire of Touchstone and Launcelot, both winners of the St. Leger in 1834 and 1840.

Touchstone, foaled in 1831, was a brown; he did not run for the Derby, but carried off the St. Leger; his dam Banter was by Master Henry, who was by Orville, grandson of King Fergus, son of Eclipse, and Banter's dam was by Alexander, son of Eclipse. Here we have an instance of considerable in-breeding to Eclipse, the direct male descendant from the Darley Arabian, through Bartlet Childers. Touchstone was the sire of Cotherstone and Orlando, winners of the Derby; of Surplice, winner of the Derby and St. Leger—the first time both races were won by the same horse after a period of 48 years, when it had been won in 1800 by Champion, son of Pot8os; and as Waxy's dam was by Herod, so was Champion's dam by Highflyer, Herod's son; of Mendicant, winner of the Oaks in 1846; of Blue Bonnet and Newminster, winners of the St. Leger in 1842 and 1851; besides of many other winners, too numerous to mention here.

Leaving Cotherstone and Surplice, who have not earned much of a reputation at the stud, but whose mares may still be useful, we must consider Touchstone's sons, Orlando and Newminster.

Orlando, a bay horse, with hind legs white, with a blaze and white nose, was very good-looking; his dam, Vulture, was by Langar out of Kite, by Bustard (son of Castrel) out of Olympia, by Sir Oliver, from Scotilla, by Anvil, who was by Herod. Scotilla's dam was Scota, by Eclipse, from Harmony, by Herod out of Rutilia, sister to Highflyer's dam. I have given the pedigree at some length, being very curious from the in-breeding of Herod. Orlando is generally supposed to have had very little of the Darley Arabian blood, which, however, is a very erroneous opinion, when it is remembered that his sire came from the Darley Arabian through *sire and dam* in direct male descent, besides by various other strains, and although his dam Vulture belonged to another family, yet in looking through the names of her progenitors we find animals tracing back to Flying Childers.

From among others he was the sire of Fazzoletto, Fitz-Roland, and Diophantus, winners of the Two Thousand Guineas; of Imperieuse, winner of the One Thousand Guineas and St. Leger; of Teddington, the winner of the Derby, 1851. Of all his sons Teddington was the most distinguished. He was a chestnut with a blaze, and a fore and hind leg white, both on the same side; he was fast, game, honest, and stout, and was one of the best examples of modern days of speed and stoutness combined; he was an excellent racehorse, won the Derby in 1851, the Doncaster Cup in 1852, and the Emperor's Plate at Ascot in 1853, beating Stockwell with great gameness; he has often been described as a short horse on a high leg; it is said he measured in girth only 63in. when he stripped for the Derby. The last time I saw him was in 1854, when he stood at Theobald's Park, Enfield. He appeared to me to be a very handsome horse, not more than 15 hands 1 inch high, with a blood-like head and eye and blood-like appearance generally, with a strong back, and very powerful quarters, which reached well forward into his middle piece, nor did he seem to me to be deficient in length; he looked as if a great stud career was before him, but his success was not very great, and his fame will rest on his own Turf performances only, I am afraid.

Orlando was also the sire of Marsyas, a finely-bred horse, his dam was Malibran by Whisker, and of Chevalier d'Industrie, whose dam was Industry (winner of the Oaks), by Priam. Teddington's dam was Miss Twickenham, by Rockingham, her dam Electress, by Election, son of Gohanna.

Newminster, a son of Touchstone and the celebrated Beeswing, being a delicate horse, was difficult to train, and ran, I believe, quite big for the St. Leger, which he won in 1851. He was a dark bay horse, without white. The young Newminsters have been chestnut, bay, brown, and grey, some large and some small. His dam, Beeswing, was by the evergreen Doctor Syntax, son of Paynator, grandson of Conductor; Doctor Syntax's dam was by Beningbrough, grandson of Eclipse; Beeswing's dam was by Ardrossan, by John Bull, son of Fortitude, who was by Herod, from a Snap mare. His son Musjid won the Derby in 1859, and Hermit in 1867, whose dam is Seclusion by Tadmor. His son, Lord Clifden, won the St. Leger in 1863, his dam The Slave, by Melbourne, her dam Volley, by Voltaire, from Martha Lynn, by Mulatto. Then there are his sons, Newcastle, Strathconan, Vespasian, and Adventurer, foaled in 1859, whose dam, Palma, was by Emilius, from Francesca, by Partizan out of a mare, by Orville (the sire of Emilius).

Adventurer has already made himself known, being the sire of Pretender, winner of the Derby in 1869. There are other descendants of both Orlando and Newminster who may still make themselves names at the stud. Before leaving the Touchstone line, although it would occupy too much space to dilate upon all his descendants, I think it only fit to mention his grandson, Dundee, who, after a very bad break down, ran second to Kettledrum for the Derby in 1861 on three legs. He was a very nice-looking horse, with fine quarters, and is a good horse to look at from behind; his shoulders have a good slope, but a little heavy at the points.

Defence, a brown horse, foaled in 1824, is the next son of Whalebone who must come under our notice. His dam was Defiance, by Rubens. His blood is as scarce as it is good, and until lately was chiefly represented through his daughters. His daughter Deception won the Oaks in 1839. His mares seemed to have mated well with horses of the Partisan line. He was the sire, Southdown and Defenceless the dams, of Alarm and Caractacus, also of Fortress, the dam of Pyrrhus the First. He was also the sire of The Emperor, a chestnut horse, foaled in 1841, winner of the Ascot Cup in 1844, and of the Emperor's Plate (Ascot) in 1845; his dam was by Reveller, and her dam, Design (own sister to Dangerous, winner of the Derby in

1833), was by Tramp out of Defiance, by Rubens; here is breeding back to the same mare—Defiance was the dam of Defence, sire of The Emperor. Tramp, the sire of The Emperor's maternal granddam, Design, was the great-grandson of Eclipse, as Defence was great-great-grandson of Eclipse. Moreover, the dam of Rubens (sire of Defiance), as has been shown before, was by Alexander, a son of Eclipse; so that there is much in-breeding to the Darley Arabian through Eclipse; but the pedigree of Defiance, paternal grandmother and maternal great-grandmother of The Emperor, goes back to Magnolia, by Marske, great-grandson of the Darley Arabian; and her great-granddam was Ebony, a daughter of Flying Childers, son of the Darley Arabian. This pedigree may be a little tedious and intricate, but it will show how that The Emperor, a great-grandson in male descent of Waxy, traced back to the Darley Arabian through most, if not all, of the female descents. Defence was the sire of Safeguard, foaled in 1841, of Grace Darling (the dam of Hero), and of Sister to Ægis, the dam of Andover, winner of the Derby, 1854.

I presume The Emperor was but lightly esteemed in this country, and therefore allowed to go to France, where he, as many others have, turned out a trump-card. He is the accepted grandsire of Gladiateur, whose dam was Miss Gladiator, a daughter of Gladiator by Partisan, another of the expatriated horses. Miss Gladiator's dam was Taffrail, by Sheet Anchor, Taffrail's dam The Warwick mare, by Merman (son of Whalebone), from a mare by Ardrossan, her dam Shepherdess, by Shuttle.

Gladiateur, a bay horse, standing about 16 hands 1½ inch, with quite a French pedigree, but from some of the best blood in England, was the first horse bred abroad who won the Epsom Derby. That he was a remarkable horse and a first-class racer few could be found to deny ; but although possessing some splendid points, that he has not that true and perfect symmetry that would be desirable in a first-rate performer and stud horse, is equally certain. I do not wish to cavil at or even find fault with a really first-class horse because he may not possess that symmetry which would be thoroughly pleasing to the eye ; but at the same time, had he been of truer shape, I have no doubt he would have been equally good in a smaller compass, and that with less of wear and tear and expenditure of power. He might be classed with that fine specimen of a race-horse, Bay Middleton. His head, eye, neck, and shoulders are truly grand ; his legs are not first-rate, nor are his quarters, to say the least, the handsomest. That he will be a stud success I both hope and expect ; and to make use of his blood to the fullest extent, and pre-eminently that of his great-grandsire, Defence, I would select for him certain mares whose dams were by Defence, or by horses whose dams were by Defence—such as mares by Alarm and by Andover (if they could be obtained), by Pyrrhus the First, and by Caractacus. Thus, as in former days, by breeding from mares whose sires were from mares by sons of Flying Childers, such as Blaze, Snip, and his son Snap, the Darley Arabian blood was brought back, and to a very great extent confirmed in Waxy; so would the Defence blood be concentrated in horses so bred.

As in the days of Waxy, it was not the engrafting the stock, or rather blood, of the Byerly Turk upon the stem of the Darley Arabian through Bartlet's Childers, but the getting back and concentrating that which had made the Turk's line truly valuable—namely, the blood of the Darley Arabian—which, as has been shown, was so strongly infused into the Turk's family through Flying Childers, which proved so great a success in Waxy.

So in the case of mating the before-mentioned mares with Gladiateur should we be confirming, perhaps, the best family of the Darley Arabian line. Daughters of Old Defenceless and any mares that there may be by Old England, whose dam Fortress was by Defence, would be well mated with him; in short, I would bring to bear as much Defence blood as could be procured to strengthen the blood that has been so nearly lost to us, but which has fortunately been restored to some extent by Gladiateur.

Gladiateur shows much of the character of his maternal grandsire, Gladiator; he has the eye of the family, which is also to be particularly noticed in the mares Vesuvienne and Harriott. This feature has doubtless resulted from the frequent infusion of the Darley Arabian's blood, particularly through Waxy.

Before leaving the Defence family I think a few words

may be devoted to Safeguard. His dam was by Selim from Euryone, who was by Witchcraft from Fair Ellen (the dam of Lilias, winner of the Oaks). Fair Ellen was by a horse styled The Wellesley Grey Arab, out of Maria, by Highflyer. Owing to his blindness, and perhaps also to the prejudice against the infusion of Eastern blood he had derived from his great-granddam, Fair Ellen, daughter of The Wellesley Grey Arab, notwithstanding she was the dam of an Oaks winner, Safeguard was not much patronised by first-class mares, and from the same source, the more recent infusion of *Eastern* blood, may be attributed his other unexceptionable qualities, wonderful constitution, and the extraordinary goodness of his feet and legs. There may not be any of his mares left now, but some of his granddaughters might make a great hit with Gladiateur if any one would venture the attempt.

The Wellesley Arab was an Eastern horse, but the Stud Book says evidently he was not an Arabian. It would be interesting to know from whence he was obtained and his antecedents before he was brought to this country.

Sir Hercules was a handsome black horse, foaled in 1826; in the autumn of the year I have heard he might have been called almost grey, from some grey hairs either becoming more numerous or more visible. He heads a very distinguished branch of the Whalebone family. He ran third for the St. Leger in 1829, Rowton and Voltaire having been first and second. His dam was Peri, by Wanderer, her dam Thalestris, a black mare, by Alexander (son of Eclipse); and Goldfinder, by Snap (grandson of Flying Childers), appears as one of her ancestors. Wanderer was by Gohanna, a grandson of Eclipse.

The pedigree of Sir Hercules shows considerable inbreeding to the Darley Arabian in direct male descent through both sire and dam; his sire and his dam's sire were both great-grandsons of Eclipse.

Sir Hercules was the sire of Coronation, winner of the Derby in 1841, a very fine horse; of Faugh a Ballagh, winner of the St. Leger in 1844, a horse of high courage, fine temper, and great power; he also won the Cesarewitch Stakes at Newmarket, beating a large field, carrying as a three-year-old 8st, The Emperor, 7st 13lb, the same age, running fourth to him, but was in his turn beaten by The Emperor the next year at Ascot for the Emperor's Plate. He was a dark brown in colour, was sent to France, and became the sire of Fille de l'Air.

Sir Hercules is principally known through his son Birdcatcher, commonly called Irish Birdcatcher, foaled in 1833, and own brother to Faugh a Ballagh; their dam Guiccoli was by Bob Booty, by Chanticleer, from a daughter of Eclipse. Bob Booty's dam, Ierne, has a curious pedigree, but of too great a length to be inserted here. It contains the names of such horses as Traveller, Hartley's Blind Horse, Darley's Arabian, Godolphin Arab, Partner, Bay Bolton, Justice, Ringtail Galloway, Litton Arab, Curwen's Bay barb, Hip, and sister to Piping Peg. Irish Birdcatcher was the sire of one Derby winner, Daniel O'Rourke, in 1852, who defeated Stockwell, grandson of Birdcatcher; of one Oaks winner, Songstress, in 1852; of three St. Leger winners: The Baron in 1845, Knight of St. George in 1854, Warlock in 1856. He was the sire of Saunterer, a black horse of great merit. For some time the latter was abroad, but was purchased by Mr. Blenkiron, and so restored to this country. He is the sire of Gamos, winner of the Oaks, with a good chance of making himself a stud reputation.

Birdcatcher was a chestnut horse; his stock had generally the reputation of being smart, light, and active, a trifle small and short, but I have seen some Birdcatchers of almost gigantic size. Nor should I say they were all systematically blood-like in appearance. Some show much quality; in others I have seen points of quite a different character. The pedigree of his dam shows, I think, more than the usual amount of indifferent breeding, although mixed with good strains, which may account for the conflicting appearances seen in his stock. His son, The Baron, winner of the St. Leger in 1845, has chiefly made him famous; he was a dark chestnut horse, with a star, a white spot at the muzzle—I think the off nostril—near hind foot white. He had a bony, prominent head, very fine shoulders, short back, and his quarters drooping a little to the setting-on of the tail, but his thighs were well let down. He won the Cesarewitch Stakes the same year, but he was defeated in the Cambridgeshire by Alarm, a horse of the same age, The Baron carrying 7st 8lb, the latter 7st 9lb. The next year The Baron did not win a single race, and was again beaten by Alarm for the Emperor's Plate at Ascot. In 1847 he went to the stud, and was located at Stockwell. His dam, Echidna, was by Economist, son of Whisker, son of Waxy; her dam, Miss Pratt, was by Blacklock, from Gadabout, by Orville, from Minstrel, by Sir Peter. Here is in-breeding to some extent to Waxy. Echidna and Birdcatcher were grandson and daughter of the own brothers, Whalebone and Whisker, sons of Waxy. The Baron, through sire and dam, was great-grandson of Waxy. The Baron was the sire of Stockwell and Rataplan, both chestnuts. Their dam, Pocahontas, was by Glencoe, son of Sultan; her dam, Marpessa, by Muley, son of Orville; her dam, Clare, by Marmion out of Harpalice, by Gohanna. Stockwell, who has been termed the 'Emperor of Stallions,' was foaled in 1849. Won the Two Thousand Guineas in 1852, was beaten by Daniel O'Rourke for the Derby, but won the St. Leger, Daniel running third. He is the sire of far too numerous a progeny to mention here; among them were two Derby winners, and the winners of six St. Legers: Blair Athol, winner of both events; Lord Lyon, also a double winner; St. Albans, Caller Ou, The Marquis, and Achievement, winners of the St. Leger.

Blair Athol, a chestnut with a white face. His dam was the celebrated Blink Bonny, by Melbourne out of the no less distinguished Queen Mary, by Gladiator. Being now at the stud, and to be seen at any time, stock can be taken of him, and his performances are too recent to need to be recapitulated. The way in which he and General Peel came away from their horses in the Derby of 1864 must be still fresh in the memory of most. St. Albans' dam was Bribery, by The Libel. Caller Ou's dam was Haricot, whose sire was Mango or Lanercost, her dam Queen Mary, by Gladiator. The Marquis was a bay horse out of Cinizelli, by Touchstone, from Brocade, by Pantaloon. Lord Lyon, a bay, and Achievement brown (own brother and sister), their dam Paradigm, by Paragone (a son of Touchstone), her dam Ellen Horne, by Redshank out of Delhi, by Plenipotentiary, are perhaps bred more directly back to Eclipse than any of the others; and though their dam may not be so illustrious as Blair Athol's, the strains they inherit through her from Catton, Emilius, and Touchstone cannot but be valuable; and I am inclined to think if Blair Athol may be generally considered the best representative of his sire, the breeding of Lord Lyon is the more perfect. The Stockwell and Touchstone cross, as it is termed, has become almost a proverb, but Beadsman would appear to be an appropriate sire for Stockwell mares. Birdcatcher was also the sire of the grey horse Chanticleer, the sire of Sunbeam (winner of the St. Leger, 1858). This brings us to the end of the Sir Hercules family, and a few words about Whisker must close the review of the Darley Arabian line through Pot8os.

Whisker (own brother to Whalebone) was the sire of Economist, the sire of Harkaway, who was the sire of King Tom,[1] from Stockwell's dam, Pocahontas, several of whose mares have been good performers, although,

[1] Kingcraft, son of King Tom, won the Derby, 1870.

with rare exceptions, his sons have not been so successful. Whisker was also the sire of The Colonel, whose son, Chatham, was the sire of the celebrated Governess.

King Fergus, a chestnut horse, foaled in 1775, is the second son of Eclipse it was proposed to notice. His two sons, Hambletonian and Beningbrough, are the fathers of two families we shall consider. From the former came the Blacklocks; the latter was the ancestor of Emilius, Priam, and Plenipotentiary. Three of his sons were winners of the St. Leger—Young Traveller, Beningbrough, and Hambletonian.

The dam of King Fergus was Tuting's Polly, by Black-and-all-Black out of his Fanny, by Tartar, from a mare by Old Starling, from a Flying Childers mare. Black-and-all-Black was by Crab, son of Alcock Arabian, from Miss Slammerkin.

Beningbrough, winner of the St. Leger in 1794, was a bay horse, from a Herod mare. He was the sire of two Oaks winners, Briseis and Oriana, and his son, Orville, won the St. Leger in 1802. Orville was a bay horse, his dam was Evelina, by Highflyer. His sons, Octavius and Emilius, were winners of the Derby, and Ebor of the St. Leger in 1817. He was also the sire of Muley, whose son, Little Wonder, carried off the Derby in 1840; his daughter, Vespa, the Oaks in 1833; and his son, Margrave, the St. Leger, in 1832. His son, Muley Moloch, was the sire of that beautiful and truly famous mare, Alice Hawthorn. She was bred back to the Darley Arabian to a very great extent; her sire was a direct male descendant through King Fergus and Eclipse, and Nancy, the dam of Muley Moloch, her sire was by Dick Andrews, a grandson in male descent of Eclipse, and her dam, Rebecca, was the offspring of collateral lines from the Darley Arabian in both male and female descents. The sire of Rebecca was Lottery, who was by Tramp, great-grandson of Eclipse, from the celebrated Mandane, a daughter of Pot8os, son of Eclipse. Rebecca's dam was by Cervantes (son of Don Quixote, who was a grandson of Eclipse), from Anticipation, by Beningbrough, the head of the branch of the King Fergus family we are now considering, and grandson of Eclipse. The breeding of these two mares, mother and daughter, is perhaps as perfect as anything that we may find since the days of the Childers.

Little Wonder was a brilliant bay in colour, and stood 14 hands 3 inches in height. He was a good and game little horse, and is one of the examples that occasionally occur which prove that speed, stride, and power are not altogether consequent upon height, size, and apparent length. The Derby of 1840 seems to have been a very true run race. They got away at an excellent pace, Little Wonder lying about seventh. After going half a mile the running was taken up by the Melody colt, Launcelot second, Little Wonder sixth. In going round the turn Little Wonder took his place at Launcelot's quarters, and these three were all that were left in the race; the others were beaten off. At the distance it was all up with the Melody colt, and Little Wonder challenged the 'crack' Launcelot, headed him in a few yards, was half a length ahead of him before they reached the Stand, and was a clever winner by a length. It must be remembered that Launcelot, who was the St. Leger winner of the year, was a horse of great speed. Little Wonder was nicely bred, but not nearly so perfect in that respect as Rebecca and Alice Hawthorn.

We must now return to Emilius (son of Orville), winner of the Derby in 1823. He was a bay horse; his dam, Emily, was by Stamford, by Sir Peter; her dam has not a very excellent pedigree, but Stamford's dam, Horatio, was by Eclipse—I think the only return to the Darley Arabian blood, but it goes by to Rib, the Wynn Arabian and Alcock Arabian—yet Sir Peter, Stamford's sire, has several strains of that blood; his dam, Papillon, was by Snap, great-grandson of the Darley Arabian. He was a very fine horse, stood about 15 hands 2 inches in height, and was considered of almost faultless symmetry. I believe he was also conspicuous for the size or depth of his back ribs, which point Mango also possessed. His sons, Priam and Plenipotentiary, were Derby winners; his daughter, Oxygen, a winner of the Oaks; and Mango, his son, won the St. Leger in 1837.

Priam, foaled in 1827, a bay horse from Cressida, sister to Eleanor, by Whiskey, has been described as a fine horse to stand up against, but narrow and light; however, he had fine action. His daughters, Miss Letty, Industry, and Crucifix, were winners of the Oaks.

Perhaps he is more distinguished as the sire of Crucifix than by anything else. She was the winner of both the Two Thousand and One Thousand Guineas, and the

Oaks; her dam Octaviana, by Octavian, her dam by Shuttle out of Zara, by Delpini from Flora, by King Fergus. Her pedigree goes back to the Darley Arabian, through Shuttle, who was by Young Marske (son of Marske, great-grandson of the Darley Arabian, and through his dam the Vauxhall Snap mare). Vauxhall Snap was by Snap, grandson of Flying Childers, and again through King Fergus, the head of the line from Eclipse we are now reviewing. Crucifix was the dam of Cowl, by Bay Middleton, Crozier by Lanercost, and Surplice by Touchstone.

Plenipotentiary, winner of the Derby in 1834, was a rich chestnut horse, a little over 15 hands 2 inches; he was a large horse, of great muscular development, and carried plenty of flesh; he won the Derby without the shadow of a struggle, and was considered one of the most magnificent horses ever seen on a racecourse. Poison, a filly of his, won the Oaks in 1843. As a sire he does not appear to have answered the expectations that his appearance might have warranted. In his pedigree the blood of the Byerly Turk, the Darley Arabian, and of the Godolphin Arab or Barb would appear to have been pretty equally distributed.

We now return to Hambletonian, winner of the St. Leger in 1795, a bay horse, his dam a Highflyer mare, her dam Monimia, by Matchem, &c. With the exception of the strains through Highflyer, we find no further return to the Darley Arabian; he was the sire of Whitelock, a bay horse from Rosalind, got by Phœnomenon, her dam Atalanta, by Matchem, with no other strain of the Darley Arabian than those through Phœnomenon, by Herod and his dam Frenzy, by Eclipse, and one through Blank, whose dam was the Little Hartley mare, by Bartlet's Childers. He was the sire of Blacklock, a bay horse, foaled in 1814; his dam was by Coriander, a son of Pot8os, her dam Wildgoose, by Highflyer out of Coheiress, by Pot8os. Coriander's dam was Lavender, by Herod from a mare by Snap out of Miss Roan, by Cade from Madam, by Bloody-Buttocks, who was a grey Arabian, with a red mark on his hip; but nothing further is known of him.

Coheiress, who was also by Pot8os, from Manilla, by Goldfinder (son of Snap) out of an Old England mare, from a mare, by the Cullen Arabian, from a mare by Cade, &c. The sire of Blacklock's dam and her granddam were by the same horse, Pot8os. This is a curious and interesting pedigree, showing a considerable amount of in-breeding to the Darley Arabian, but much mingled with other inferior strains. Blacklock's most memorable race was four miles, at York, when he defeated Magistrate by a short head, but it finished both of them; he was a plain, coarse horse, with bad fore legs. His son, Velocipede, foaled in 1825, was a chestnut horse, his dam was by Juniper, son of Whiskey (grandson of Eclipse), her dam by Sorcerer, son of Trumpator of the Godolphin Arabian's line out of Virgin, by Sir Peter out of a mare by Pot8os out of Editha, by Herod from Elfrida, by Snap. He was highly esteemed by John Scott, and was the sire of Amato, winner of the Derby in 1838, and also of the Queen of Trumps, a slashing brown mare, winner of the Oaks and St. Leger in 1835. She had great speed, like her sire, and like him I should say doubtful legs; her dam was Princess Royal, by Castrel. Blacklock was also the sire of Brutandorf, sire of Hetman Platoff, the sire of Cossack, winner of the Derby in 1847. Brutandorf's dam was Mandane, by Pot8os. Cossack, a chestnut horse, was from a Priam mare. Voltaire, by Blacklock, was a brown horse, foaled in 1826, and his descendants are mostly dark brown or black; his dam was a Phantom mare, and traces back to Matchem; he was the sire of Charles XII., who won the St. Leger after a dead heat with Euclid, a son of Emilius, and also the sire of Voltigeur, winner of the Derby and St. Leger in 1850; the latter race was won after a dead heat with Russborough; he also won the Doncaster Cup the same week, defeating the, up to that time, unconquered Flying Dutchman, but he was subsequently defeated by The Dutchman in a two-mile match at York. His dam was Martha Lynn, by Mulatto, son of Catton out of the Mercury line from Eclipse. Mulatto's dam was by Orville; there is considerable breeding back to Eclipse in his pedigree. From among many others, Voltigeur was the sire of Vedette, Skirmisher, and Sabreur; but, to my mind, Buckstone was his best son, a bay or brown horse, foaled in France in 1859; his dam was Burlesque by Touchstone, her dam, Maid of Honour, by Champion out of Etiquette, by Orville, which gives more breeding back to Eclipse. He ran third to Caractacus for the Derby in 1862, and second to The Marquis for The St. Leger. He was generally considered a horse with two good ends, but deficient in middle piece; but I thought him a fine horse when he ran with Tim Whiffler for the Ascot Cup, which he won after a dead heat. It was a sight worth seeing in these days. He was sent out to China in 1863, and died there.

Voltigeur's memory and likeness will probably be preserved, as Sir Edwin Landseer has depicted him on canvas with his cat almost, if not quite, as large as life.

This must suffice for the King Fergus family, and we will get back to the year 1778, when the chestnut horse, Mercury, son of Eclipse, was foaled; his dam was by Tartar, great-grandson of the Byerly Turk, her dam by Mogul, son of the Godolphin Arab or Barb, without any return to the Darley Arabian. He was the sire of Gohanna, a bay horse, foaled in 1790; his dam was a Herod mare, her dam, Maiden Sister to Pumpkin, by Matchem, from a mare by Squirt, her dam by Mogul out of Camilla, by Bay Bolton from Old Lady, by Pulleine's chestnut Arabian from a mare by Rockwood from a mare by Bustler. There are strains here of the Darley Arabian, through his dam by Herod and through Pumpkin's dam, but there are many strains containing other than Eastern blood. He was the sire of Golumpus, a bay horse, foaled in 1802; his dam, Catherine, by Woodpecker, her dam, Camilla, by Trentham. This latter horse was by Sweepstakes from Miss South, her dam by Cartouch out of Ebony, by Flying Childers. Woodpecker and Ebony gave him some of the Darley Arabian blood, but there is much of the Godolphin

Arab or Barb's, and many strains of inferior blood. He was the sire of Catton, a bay horse, foaled in 1809; he was the first foal of Lucy Gray, whose sire was Timothy, her dam Lucy, by Florizel out of Frenzy, by Eclipse. Through Lucy and Florizel (son of Herod) he inherited rather more of the Darley Arabian blood. Florizel's dam was a daughter of Cygnet, by the Godolphin Arab or Barb, from a daughter of Crab (son of Alcock's Arab), from a daughter of Flying Childers; Cygnet's dam was by Cartouch, from Ebony, by Flying Childers out of Old Ebony, by Basto, and Basto, one of the very few horses altogether of Eastern blood; but he was not like the Childers of Arabian blood on the sire's side. Basto was by the Byerly Turk out of Bay Peg, who was by the Leedes Arabian out of Young Bald Peg, who was by the Leedes Arabian out of Spanker's dam, which was the old Morocco mare, by the Morocco Barb out of Old Bald Peg, who was by an Arabian out of a Barb mare. The Childers were by the Darley Arabian out of Betty Leedes, who was by Careless out of Sister to Leedes, who was by the Leedes Arabian, out of a mare by Spanker, out of a Barb mare, which was Spanker's dam, viz., the old Morocco mare, by the Morocco Barb out of Bald Peg, who was by an Arabian out of a Barb mare. Careless, the sire of Betty Leedes, was by Spanker out of a Barb mare, and Spanker was by D'Arcy's Yellow Turk out of the above old Morocco mare. Catton was a stout horse, with capital legs. It will be seen besides the strains of blood going back to the Darley Arabian, there was very much in breeding on his dam's side through Basto, to the Childers through their dam, Betty Leedes. Catton was the sire of Mulatto (the sire of Voltigeur's dam), and Mulatto was the sire of Bloomsbury (winner of the Derby in 1839). Catton was the sire of Mundig, out of Emma, by Whisker, winner of the Derby, 1835, a horse with splendid action, especially when he got well into his stride; of Tarrare, winner of the St. Leger, 1826; of Royal Oak, who was the sire of Slane, who was the sire of that fine-looking horse Merry Monarch, winner of the Derby, 1845; and of Princess, winner of the Oaks, 1844. Slane himself ran fourth for the Derby, 1836, won by Bay Middleton, Gladiator and Venison being second and third. He was a rich bay in colour, and was the sire of Queen Anne, the dam of Kingston; his dam was an Orville mare, and strained back to King Fergus and Marske through Alexina, the granddam of the Orville mare. Slane was sold and went abroad. Catton was also the sire of Sandbeck, a bay horse, foaled in 1818, his dam was Orvillina, sister to Orville. Sandbeck was the sire of Barbelle, the dam of Van Tromp and The Flying Dutchman. There is considerable breeding back to Darley Arabian both in Sandbeck and in Barbelle, whose dam, Darioletta, was by Amadis, son of Don Quixote (brother to Alexander), by Eclipse; and her dam Selima was out of a mare by Pot8os (by Eclipse) from Editha, by Herod out of Elfrida, by Snap, great-grandson of the Darley Arabian. She had springy, elastic action, which was bequeathed to her son, The Flying Dutchman, and to several of his sons, certainly no small recommendation to racing stock. The line from the Darley Arabian will be lastly traced through Joe Andrews.

The fourth and last son of Eclipse whose descendants we shall trace is Joe Andrews (at first called Dennis O!), a bay horse. His dam was Amaranda, by Omnium; her dam Cloudy, by Blank out of Fancy, a grey mare by Crab (son of Alcock's Arab); her dam Spinster (the Widdrington mare), who was by Partner out of bay Bloody-Buttocks, by the Arab Bloody-Buttocks. Omnium, sire of Amaranda, was by Snap, great-grandson of the Darley Arabian from Miss Cade; her dam by Partner out of a mare by Makeless (son of the Oglethorpe Arabian and a mare by Brimmer, son of D'Arcy's Yellow Turk and a Royal mare) out of a mare by Place's White Turk, out of a mare by Dodsworth out of the Layton Barb mare.

Besides being in direct male descent from the Darley Arabian, Joe Andrews got two other strains of that blood, one through Omnium, the other through Cloudy, whose dam was the Little Hartley mare by Bartlet's Childers. There are numerous other strains of Eastern blood, with perhaps fewer flaws than is usually the case.

Dick Andrews, his son (foaled in 1794), was a bay horse; his dam a Highflyer mare; her dam by Cardinal Puff out of a mare by Tatler out of Bay Snip, by Snip (son of Flying Childers), out of a mare by the Godolphin Arab or Barb, out of Frampton's Whiteneck, full sister to the Mixbury Galloway. Cardinal Puff, a grey horse, was by Babraham out of a mare by Snip; her dam Lady Thigh, by Partner out of a mare by Bloody-

Buttocks (own sister to the dam of the Widdrington mare). Tatler was by Blank out of a mare by Partner out of Bonny Lass, by Bolton from a Darley Arabian mare. This pedigree shows in-breeding to the Arab Bloody-Buttocks, and some strains of the Darley Arabian, with several of the Godolphin Arab's and Byerly Turk's blood, but prior to the infusions of the Darley Arabian blood into the Byerly Turk's line, which it is believed so greatly enhanced its value.

Tramp, son of Dick Andrews, a bay horse, foaled in 1810; his dam a Gohanna mare from Fraxinella, by Trentham from a Woodpecker mare out of Everlasting, who was by Eclipse out of Hyæna, by Snap (great-grandson of the Darley Arabian), thus straining back to Eclipse through Gohanna and Everlasting, and to the Darley Arabian through Hyæna, with the additional strains he would get from Woodpecker, through his sire's, Herod, dam. Tramp was the sire of two winners of the Derby, St. Giles in 1832, and Dangerous in 1833; of one St. Leger winner, Barefoot, in 1823. He was also the sire of Lottery and Liverpool; the latter horse was the sire of Lanercost. Tramp has been described as a narrow horse, but with years he came very large of bone.

The dam of Liverpool was by Whisker out of Mandane, by Pot8os out of Young Camilla, by Woodpecker. Lanercost's dam was Otis, by Bustard (son of Buzzard) out of a mare by Election. He was a gross and sluggish horse; won the Cambridgeshire in 1839, Newcastle Cup in 1840, the Ascot Cup in 1841. He was the sire of Van Tromp, the winner of the St. Leger 1847; of Catharine Hayes, winner of the Oaks 1853; of Loup-Garou, and Beauty the dam of Nutbush. His success at the stud was hardly so great as was expected; perhaps he was at first too freely used—not an unfrequent occurrence. As a racer I question if he could be considered first-rate, although he was a stout horse, which may have been owing to his infirmity, for he was tender-footed, and perhaps too ponderous for his legs. Lanercost was the sire of Ellerdale, who was the dam of Ellington (son of The Flying Dutchman), winner of the Derby 1856; and Ellermire, her daughter by Chanticleer, was the dam of Elland by Rataplan; and Liverpool was the sire of Espoir, the dam of the Oaks winner, Brown Duchess. Colsterdale, a son of Lanercost, who was at one time thought very highly of, has left a good horse to the credit of the Lanercost line, namely, Little Lecturer, whose dam Algebra was by Mathematician.

Lottery, by Tramp, a brown horse, foaled in 1820, was the winner of the Doncaster Cup in 1825, perhaps his best race. His dam was Mandane by Pot8os. He was the sire of Sheet Anchor, a brown horse, foaled in 1832. His dam was Morgiana, by Muley (son of Orville) from a mare by Sorcerer.

Weatherbit, his son, was a bay, or rather, I should say, a brown horse, foaled in 1842. His dam was Miss Letty, winner of the Oaks in 1837, a daughter of Priam; her dam by Orville from a mare by Buzzard out of Hornpipe, by Trumpator, out of Luna, by Herod; her dam, Proserpine, own sister to Eclipse. There is very considerable in-breeding to the Darley Arabian. The sire and dam of Weatherbit's sire, and the sire and dam of Miss Letty, his dam, are all descendants in male descent of sons of Eclipse. The coarseness that existed in many of his progenitors in the male line was not seen in him. Even when old and infirm he was a very good-looking horse, with a level top and high quarters, good hocks, and well-shaped and well-placed hind legs. He has left several sons. From among them, Bel Demonio, from a Birdcatcher mare; Bismark, also from a Birdcatcher mare; Brown Bread, from a West Australian mare; Jupiter, from Athena Pallas; Mandrake, from a mare by Rataplan. And he was also the sire of Beadsman, whose name would have been more properly written *Bedesman*.

Beadsman,[1] winner of the Derby, 1858, is a brown horse; his dam Mendicant (winner of the Oaks, 1846), by Touchstone; her dam Lady Moore Carew, by Tramp out of Kite, by Bustard (son of Castrel), her dam Olympia, by Sir Oliver (son of Sir Peter) out of Scotilla, by Anvil, from Scota, a daughter of Eclipse. Through his dam, Beadsman is in-bred to his paternal ancestor Tramp, and there is very much breeding back to the Darley Arabian on both sides of his pedigree, and although there are several strains of the blood of the Byerly Turk's line, yet they also contain much of the Darley Arabian blood. Bustard's dam, Miss Hap, was by Shuttle, by Young Marske (whose sire Marske was great-grandson of the Darley Arabian), out of the

[1] Since dead.

Vauxhall Snap mare, by Vauxhall Snap, whose sire Snap was great-grandson of the Darley Arabian. The dam of Miss Hap was sister to Haphazard, who was by Sir Peter, from an Eclipse mare, and Sir Peter's dam was Papillon, by Snap. Anvil has two strains of the Darley Arabian, besides those through the dam of his sire Herod, and both through Flying Childers. Again, the dam of Castrel (sire of Bustard and grandsire of Kite) was the Alexander mare, whose sire was by Eclipse. On the whole, Beadsman is certainly a blood-like looking horse, and had fine action. He is the sire of Blue Gown and Pero Gomez.

Blue Gown (son of Beadsman and Bas Bleu), winner of the Derby, 1868, is a bay horse. Perhaps not particularly taking in his slower paces, but a fine mover when at speed, he must be considered as a remarkably well-bred horse. We have seen that his progenitors for five generations were bred back to the Darley Arabian by several collateral lines in male descent. Thus Beadsman sprang from a union of the Joe Andrews and Waxy lines; his sire Weatherbit from a combination of the blood from Joe Andrews and King Fergus, his grandsire Sheet Anchor also from the Joe Andrews and King Fergus lines; his great-grandsire Lottery from a union of the lines from Joe Andrews and Waxy; and in some instances the dams of several of these horses were themselves bred on both sides of their pedigree from collateral and identical lines from the Darley Arabian. For instance, Miss Letty, the dam of Weatherbit, was the offspring of a horse and mare in direct male descent from King Fergus through Orville; and Mendicant, Beadsman's dam, on her sire's side came from the collateral line from Waxy, and on the side of her dam from the identical line from which her son was descended in male descent, which was that from Joe Andrews; Tramp being great-grandsire of Weatherbit and maternal grandsire of Mendicant. The inbreeding and breeding back were further prosecuted in Blue Gown. From his sire he inherited strains of the Darley Arabian blood through Joe Andrews, King Fergus, Pot8os, and Waxy, and through his dam he got a double infusion of the same blood (the Darley Arabian's) through two collateral branches of the Waxy family, she being the offspring of a descendant of Sir Hercules on her sire's side, and a descendant of Camel on the side of her dam; Sir Hercules and Camel being both grandsons of Waxy. Bas Bleu, the dam of Blue Gown, was a bay mare by Stockwell from Vexation, by Touchstone out of Vat, by Langar out of Wire (sister to Whalebone), a daughter of Waxy, and Touchstone's dam was by Master Henry, son of Orville; which gives two other additional strains from the Darley Arabian in direct male descent. In addition to his being so finely bred a horse, I think it will be generally allowed he was a good racer; and although neither his owner nor his trainer, so it has been reported, thought very highly of him, and preferred his half-brother, Rosicrucian, yet his jockey had formed quite a different opinion, and stuck to him through good and evil report; for myself, I think Blue Gown had all the appearance of a racehorse, and the other was only a handsome coach horse in comparison.

Pero Gomez, by Beadsman, ran second to Pretender for the Derby, 1869, and carried off the St. Leger; his dam Salamanca was by Student; her dam Bravery, by Gameboy out of Ennui, by Bay Middleton. This horse is to a certain extent similarly bred to his half-brother Blue Gown, but the breeding is not so perfect, the breeding back not so continuous; and although he possessed through his dam several strains of the Darley Arabian blood, the pedigree is, as it were, more broken up Student, the sire of Salamanca, is descended from Waxy through Chatham and The Colonel, and Student's dam, the Laurel mare, was from Flight by Velocipede (son of Blacklock), and Laurel was by Blacklock out of a mare by Prime Minister (son of Sancho, grandson of Eclipse) out of an Orville mare. It must have been most gratifying to the owner of Beadsman to have bred and possessed in two successive years two such horses as Blue Gown and Pero Gomez. I consider the former as far superior, and likely to be the better horse at the stud; and, as is not unusual, the more valuable blood has gone abroad, perhaps to be repurchased at some future time for this country; but such opportunities cannot always be counted upon.

We have now considered the descendants of the four sons of Eclipse, who have been principally concerned in handing down the blood of the Darley Arabian. In the earlier stages there was very little breeding back to the founder of the line, and the horses would appear, in most instances, to have possessed very considerable coarseness in appearance; but as soon as any amount of breeding back to the Darley Arabian had taken place, improvement in both *form* and appearance was discernible. In the line through Pot8os, the blood was returned to, and confirmed to a great extent in Waxy. And we have seen that the Joe Andrews line, for the last six generations, has been bred *in and in* to the Darley Arabian blood; we saw also the advantages derived from the system by such results as Rebecca, Alice Hawthorn, and Little Wonder; and quite recently by the uniting of the lines from Waxy by the breeding from Stockwell and Touchstone mares, or mares of Touchstone blood. It is not from the fact of the mares being daughters or granddaughters of Touchstone that so good a result was obtained, but that by such a union the blood of the Darley Arabian was being made more use of, was being concentrated, and through good lines and individuals.

Lord Lyon, so bred, running first in the Derby and St. Leger to Savernake and Rustic, his half-brothers, both being by Stockwell, but from mares who were not bred from collateral lines from the Darley Arabian, is an example of the good results of this system of breeding, and it is seen to a still greater extent in Blue Gown and Beadsman. Bribery, the dam of Savernake, was by The Libel (son of Pantaloon); Village Lass, the dam of Rustic, was by Pyrrhus the First, and although both inherited strains of the Darley Arabian's blood on their dams' side, they were not in-bred through collateral lines.

The line from Mercury can hardly be said to be represented now; that from King Fergus principally by Voltigeur and his sons; the Pot8os and Waxy line principally by the Birdcatchers, Stockwells, and Newminsters, with still some Touchstones and Orlandos, and now again through Defence, as the services of his grand representative Gladiateur have been available for breeders in this country. I shall be surprised if Lord Lyon does not leave his mark at the stud if he has a fair chance, and perhaps his mares may hereafter be especially well mated to the representatives of the Joe Andrews line.

The line through this fourth son of Eclipse from the Darley Arabian has been splendidly bred up for some generations; and although the representatives are not so numerous as those of the Pot8os and Waxy line, the excellence of the breeding of Beadsman and Blue Gown is not to be surpassed by any of the Waxy lines. There are also several of Weatherbit's sons at the stud; and Lecturer may also do some service for the line from which he has sprung; he is in good hands.

Some further remarks will be offered on the subject of this grand source from which our racehorse has sprung when the whole review shall have been completed. The Godolphin Arab or Barb and his descendants will next be considered.

The Line from the Godolphin Arab or Barb.

The Godolphin Arab or Barb, the head of the third line of our English racers, was a dark bay or brown bay horse, said to have been about 15 hands high. He is supposed to date back to 1724, but was first used as a stallion in this country in 1731. In all probability nothing certain will now be known of his origin. I understand the distinguished Turkish general, Omar Pasha, who made enquiries about him, was informed in Egypt that he was of the breed or family called Jelfan, which would lead to the supposition that he had either passed from Arabia through Egypt into Africa, or as there was no distinctive name attached to the generic of Jelfan, that he might have been foaled in Egypt, got by a horse of the Jelfan family, from a mare of Egypt; for had he been pure Arabian of the Jelfan family, the distinguishing adjunct would in all probability have been also known, and he may have been brought from thence or some other part of Northern Africa into Europe. There is a story current in France that he had been sent over as a present to the King of France, which would have been Louis XV., but by whom is not mentioned; probably the story had its origin in, or was confounded with, the history of the Curwen Bay Barb, presented to Louis XIV. The original portrait of the Godolphin Arab or Barb I have not seen. All of the prints of him do not correspond; but the expression of the countenance, and the outline of the head as more generally depicted, would lead to the supposition that he was a horse of Northern Africa (commonly called a Barb), and not of pure or unmixed Arabian blood, which surmise would be further strengthened by the drawing of the ears, which are shown as lopping outwards. The first of his get was Lath, foaled in 1731, whose dam was Roxana, by the Bald Galloway; he was also the sire of Regulus, foaled in 1739, whose dam, Grey Robinson, was by the Bald Galloway; and Regulus was the sire of Spiletta, dam of Eclipse. The Godolphin Arab or Barb was also the sire of the Gower stallion, Babraham, and Blank, but his line in male descent is handed down for some time through a single string of horses—Cade, Matchem, Conductor, and Trumpator; and then the line divides. Paynator and Sorcerer, sons of the last-named horse, formed two branches; that from Paynator is carried on in single line, while Sorcerer formed three branches, headed by Smolensko, Soothsayer, and Comus.

Cade, by the Godolphin Arab or Barb, was a bay horse; his dam Roxana, got by the Bald Galloway; her dam Sister to Chanter, by the Akaster Turk, from a mare by the Leedes Arabian, whose dam was by Spanker. The Bald Galloway was by St. Victor's Barb out of a mare by Why Not, from a Royal mare.

Matchem, a bay horse, by Cade out of a mare by Partner (grandson of the Byerly Turk); her dam by Makeless out of a mare by Brimmer, from a mare by Place's White Turk out of a mare by Dodsworth, out of the Layton Barb mare. He was the sire of Teetotum (winner of the Oaks, 1780), and of Hollandaise (winner of the St. Leger, 1778). In Matchem there is the first direct union of the Godolphin Arab or Barb's line with that of the Byerly Turk.

Conductor, a chestnut horse, foaled 1767, by Matchem; his dam by Snap (grandson of Flying Childers); her dam by the Cullen Arabian out of Lady Thigh, by Partner. Here we have the blood of the Darley Arabian introduced for the first time with another strain of the Byerly Turk's blood.

Trumpator, by Conductor, foaled in 1782, was a black horse, from whom are descended several horses of the same colour; his dam was Brunette, a mare combining the blood of the Byerly Turk and of the Godolphin Arab or Barb, with a distant strain or two of the Darley Arabian's. Brunette was by Squirrel, a speedy horse (by Old Traveller), son of Partner, out of a mare by Almanzor (a remarkably fine horse by the Darley Arabian); Squirrel's dam was by the Arab Bloody-Buttocks.

Dove, the dam of Brunette, was by Matchless (son of the Godolphin Arab or Barb, out of South's dam, by Soreheels), son of Basto, a horse of Eastern blood, whose breeding on his dam's side was very similar to that of the Childers on the side of their dam. Dove's dam was by the Ancaster Starling, granddam by Grasshopper, great-granddam by Sir M. Newton's Arabian. The line here branches into two descents. That through Paynator will be taken first.

Paynator, by Trumpator, a brown colt, foaled in 1791; his dam was by Mark Anthony, son of Spectator, son of Crab, by the Alcock's Arab, out of Signora, by Snap (great-grandson of the Darley Arabian), out of Miss Windsor, by the Godolphin Arab or Barb, through whom one other strain of the Darley Arabian was inherited from a mare by Bartlet's Childers.

From Paynator came the evergreen Doctor Syntax, foaled in 1811, the first foal of a mare by Beningbrough, and being small was very nearly being devoted to other purposes than that of the sire of racehorses. The dam of the Beningbrough mare, Jenny Mole, was by Carbuncle, a son of Babraham Blank (grandson of the Godolphin Arab or Barb), out of a mare by Prince T'Quassaw (a son of Snip, grandson of the Darley Arabian), out of Dairymaid, by the Arab Bloody-Buttocks out of a mare by Regulus (son of the Godolphin Arab or Barb), out of a mare by Partner, grandson of the Byerly Turk. Babraham Blank was by Babraham out of Sister to Blank, by the Godolphin Arab or Barb out of the Little Hartley mare (a daughter of Bartlet's Childers). This is an uncommon and curious pedigree, containing a good amount of the Darley Arabian's blood, some of the Byerly Turk's, but much in-breeding to the Godolphin Arab.

The Doctor, a black horse, foaled in 1834, son of Doctor Syntax, ran third to Mango for the St. Leger. His dam was by Lottery from Elizabeth, by Walton out of Trulla, by Sorcerer, granddam by Weathercock out of Cade, by Matchem. He was the sire of The Black Doctor, a black horse, foaled in 1848, whose dam, Betsy Bird, was by Voltaire out of Zephyrina, by Middlethorpe out of Pagoda, by Sir Peter. Middlethorpe, a chestnut horse, was by Shuttle (by Young Marske, great-grandson of Bartlet's Childers out of the Vauxhall Snap mare). He had a great many strains of the Darley Arabian blood, and was also bred back by several strains to the Godolphin Arab or Barb. He won the Manchester Trade Cup in 1852, then four years old, carrying 8st. 3lb. He was a good-looking horse, with much

Arabian character in his head and ears, and in the swell of the barrel behind the arms. He was, however, an entire failure at the stud; although he covered his mares with much apparent vigour and determination, very few foals were accredited to him. Perhaps had he gone abroad he might have done better. Sabreur's was a very similar case, but he begets foals in Hungary.

Perhaps the Paynator family is most celebrated by Beeswing, a bay mare, by Doctor Syntax, and dam of Newminster. She was foaled in 1833. Her dam was by Ardrossan out of Lady Eliza, by Whitworth out of a mare by Spadille out of Sylvia, by Young Marske. Her pedigree on the side of her dam contains many strains of blood from the Byerly Turk's line, but also goes back to the Darley Arabian. She was six times the winner of the Newcastle Cup, and won the Ascot Cup in 1842.

We must return to Trumpator, who was the sire of Didelot, winner of the Derby 1796, from a mare by Highflyer, and of Sorcerer, a black horse (foaled in 1796), whose dam was Young Giantess, got by Diomed (the winner of the first Derby), son of Florizel. Excepting through the Cygnet mare, who was the dam of Florizel—her granddam was Ebony, by Childers—and through Herod (Florizel's sire), there is little or no return to the Darley Arabian blood; the dam of Young Giantess being Giantess, by Matchem out of Molly Longlegs, by Babraham (son of the Godolphin Arab or Barb). Soothsayer, son of Sorcerer, was a chestnut horse (foaled in 1808); he won the St. Leger in 1811; his dam Goldenlocks was by Delpini (son of Highflyer), from Violet, by Shark, a son of Marske (great-grandson of the Darley Arabian), from a mare by Snap, also his great-grandson, and the dam of Violet was by Syphon, a son of Squirt, son of Bartlet's Childers, and grandson of the Darley Arabian, out of Charlotte, by Blank (son of the Godolphin Arab or Barb, from the Little Hartley mare, by Bartlet's Childers), from a mare by Crab (son of Alcock's Arab), from a mare by Dyer's Dimple, who was by the Leedes Arabian, from a mare by Spanker, which latter horse was entirely of Eastern blood. Although there are many flaws in this pedigree, and not unfrequent returns to the Godolphin Arab or Barb's blood, yet there are very many strains of the Darley Arabians with some of the other Arab horses. His daughters, Morel and Maid of Orleans, were winners of the Oaks in 1808 and 1809, and Sorcery in 1811. Morel's dam was by Buzzard; the dam of Maid of Orleans (sister to Champion, the first winner of both Derby and St. Leger) was by Pot8os; Pot8os was a son of Eclipse.

Soothsayer was the sire of Tiresias, winner of the Derby in 1819, a brown horse, whose dam Pledge was by Waxy, of the Darley Arabian line, from Prunella, by Highflyer out of Promise, by Snap, great-grandson of the Darley Arabian, from Julia, by Blank (son of the Godolphin Arab or Barb and the Little Hartley mare, by Bartlet's Childers).

Comus and Smolensko, the sons of Sorcerer, and their descendants, will now be considered, and although

Comus is senior to the former by one year, the order of precedence will be broken for the first time, and Smolensko taken first, as the line from Comus will bring us down to a later period.

Smolensko was a black horse, foaled in 1810; winner of the Derby in 1813; his dam was Wowski, by Mentor out of Waxy's dam, by Herod out of Lisette, by Snap (grandson of Flying Childers) out of Miss Windsor, by the Godolphin Arab or Barb out of a mare by Young Belgrade, from a mare by Bartlet's Childers. Smolensko was the sire of Gulnare, winner of the Oaks in 1827, and of Jerry, winner of the St. Leger in 1824.

Jerry was a black horse, foaled in 1821; his dam Louisa by Orville, son of Beningbrough, of the King Fergus line, from Eclipse; her dam Tomasina, by Timothy out of Violet, by Shark, &c., as in the pedigree of Soothsayer. He was the sire of Tomboy, a bay horse, foaled in 1829, who in his turn was the sire of Nutwith, winner of the St. Leger in 1843. Nutwith's dam was by Comus (son of Sorcerer). Jerry was also the sire of Jericho, and Nutwith of Knight of Kars.

Comus, by Sorcerer, was a chestnut horse, foaled in 1809; his dam was Houghton Lass, by Sir Peter; her dam Alexina, by King Fergus (son of Eclipse) out of Lardella, by Young Marske out of a mare by Cade.

He was the sire of Reveller, winner of the St. Leger, 1818; of Matilda, winner of the St. Leger, 1827; and of Humphrey Clinker.

Reveller was a bay horse; his dam Rosette was by Beningbrough, of the King Fergus line.

Humphrey Clinker, a bay horse, foaled in 1822; his dam Clinkerina was by Clinker out of Pewet, by Tandem out of Termagant, by Tantrum. Clinker was by Sir Peter. Tantrum, the sire of Termagant, was by Cripple, from a mare by the Hampton Court Childers (son of Flying Childers) out of a mare by Whitefoot, from a mare by Stanyoa's Arabian, from the Moonah Barb mare. The dam of Termagant was Cantatrice, by Sampson (son of Blaze, son of Flying Childers) out of a mare by Regulus (son of the Godolphin Arab or Barb). Cripple, the sire of Tantrum, was by the Godolphin Arab or Barb out of Blossom, got by Crab (son of Alcock's Arab) out of a mare by Flying Childers. Humphrey Clinker was bred back to the founder of his line, the Godolphin Arab or Barb, but he had a great many strains of the Darley Arabian's blood.

He was the sire of Rockingham, winner of the St. Leger, 1833, and of Melbourne, a brown horse foaled in 1834. Although of no reputation as a racer, Melbourne was more successful at the stud, and by having been the sire of more winners of great events than any of his predecessors did much to establish the *popularity* of his line.

His dam was by Cervantes, from a mare by Golumpus (son of Gohanna, a direct male descendant of the Darley Arabian through Eclipse), from a mare by Paynator (son of Trumpator). Cervantes was by Don Quixote (son or grandson of Eclipse) from Evelina, by Highflyer out of Termagant, by Tantrum out of a mare by Sampson (grandson of Flying Childers)—similar breeding to that seen in the pedigree of Clinkerina (the dam of his sire Humphrey Clinker). Although he traces back through his dam to some extent to the Godolphin Arab or Barb, the strains of the Darley Arabian's blood are considerably increased.

Melbourne was the sire of Sir Tatton Sykes, who just missed the Derby, but won the St. Leger in 1846; of Cymba, winner of the Oaks, 1848; of West Australian, winner of the Two Thousand Guineas, Derby, and St. Leger in 1853 (the first time the three races had been won by the same horse); of Marchioness, winner of the Oaks, 1855; and of Blink Bonny, the winner of the Derby and Oaks in 1857, and afterwards the dam of Blair Athol.

The dam of Sir Tatton Sykes was by Margrave (son of Muley), tracing up to the Darley Arabian through Beningbrough, Gohanna, Mercury, and Eclipse, in direct male descent, besides through many other strains, but she was also bred back to the Godolphin Arab or Barb, through his descendants Sorcerer and Soothsayer.

The dam of Cymba was Skiff, by Sheet Anchor out of Tertia, by Emilius out of Miss Wentworth, by Cervantes; all in direct male descent from the Darley Arabian.

The dam of Marchioness was Cinizelli, by Touchstone, a horse through sire and dam a direct descendant of the Darley Arabian.

The dam of Blink Bonny was Queen Mary (got by Gladiator); her dam by Plenipotentiary out of Myrrha, by Whalebone. The dam of Queen Mary was in direct descent from the Darley Arabian through sire and dam, and Gladiator (son of Partisan) strained back to the Darley Arabian in two separate lines through Pot8os and Waxy, besides through numerous other channels.

West Australian, a bay horse, with a white mark down his face, foaled in 1850; his dam, Mowerina (sister to Cotherstone, winner of the Derby, 1843), was by Touchstone, a horse in-bred to the Darley Arabian through sire and dam, out of Emma by Whisker (son of Waxy out of Penelope, by Trumpator out of Prunella, by Highflyer out of Promise), by Snap (grandson of Flying Childers); and Emma's dam, Gibside Fairy, was by Hermes, son of Mercury, son of Eclipse, from Vicissitude, granddaughter of Trumpator (descendant of the Godolphin Arab or Barb), out of Beatrice by Sir Peter Melbourne was also the sire of Oulston, whose dam was Alice Hawthorn; of The Prime Minister, whose dam was by Pantaloon; and of Young Melbourne, who, again, is the sire of General Peel, whose dam was by Orlando, from Brown Bess by Camel.

West Australian was bought by Count De Morny, and went to France, and notwithstanding the many strains of fine blood he inherited, and his brilliant success as a racehorse, I do not consider his exportation to have been any loss to this country.

The line from the Godolphin Arab or Barb is principally represented by the following horses, and through the branch from Humphrey Clinker and Melbourne—The Prime Minister, Arthur Wellesley, Cannobie, Oulston, Mentmore, and Young Melbourne.

Melbourne's son, West Australian, has given Bonnyfield, Joskin, and Solon; and Young Melbourne, Rapid Rhone and General Peel. It is noteworthy how very few winners, comparatively speaking, of great events have been given by this third source from whence our racehorse has sprung; and, again, those horses, with the exception of Soothsayer and Smolensko, who have been winners themselves of one of the great events, have not begotten winners of such races. Jerry, Rockingham, Sir Tatton Sykes, and West Australian, winners of the Derby or St. Leger, have not produced winners of those events. In the cases of Soothsayer and Smolensko, as has been shown, they had several strains of the Darley Arabian blood, particularly the former horse, but none very direct; for instance, their dams were not themselves descendants, on the male side, from the Darley Arabian, but most of the winners have been bred on their dams' sides direct to the Darley Arab. Thus the dam of Tiresias, winner of the Derby, 1819, was a daughter of Waxy; her granddam Promise by Snap, with another strain through the Little Hartley mare. Jerry's dam was a daughter of Orville, in direct descent to the Darley Arabian through King Fergus, besides other strains. The dam of Reveller, winner of the St. Leger, 1819, was a daughter of Beningbrough, also a direct descendant of the Darley Arabian through King Fergus. The dam of Matilda (winner of the St. Leger, 1827), Juliana, formerly Lady Thigh, was a daughter of Gohanna; and her dam, Platina, was a daughter of Mercury (sire of Gohanna) thus going up by a double strain to the Darley Arabian through Mercury. Sir Tatton Sykes's dam was a daughter of Margrave (himself a St. Leger winner), a descendant of the Darley Arabian through the two collateral lines of King Fergus and Mercury. Cymba and Marchioness, winners of the Oaks, were almost altogether of Darley Arabian blood on the side of their dams. The granddam of Blink Bonny was also similarly bred, and West Australian's dam was a Touchstone mare, and almost entirely of Darley Arabian blood. General Peel, who ran second to Blair Athol for the Derby and St. Leger, was the son of a mare descended through sire and dam in direct male descent from the Darley Arabian.

In itself I cannot help considering the line from the Godolphin Arab or Barb a very poor one, and, like that from the Byerly Turk, it really owes what celebrity it may have, and its continuance, to the infusions of blood it has received from the descendants of the Darley Arabian. It is worthy of remark, although not extraordinary, that almost in proportion to the amount of Darley Arabian blood has been the success of the individuals of this line. This, I think, can hardly fail to strike those who may have had the patience to go so far with us; yet the many strains of fine blood inherited by most of the great winners of this line—although without doubt it was *that blood*, namely, the Darley Arabian's, which constituted their goodness and insured their success—have not enabled them to beget stock as good or successful as themselves, and to hand down a continuous line of winners. This would go very far to prove the theory correct, that should there be any difference of breeding between the sires and dams the sire should be of the purer blood. The breeding of West Australian on his dam's side being so superior and overwhelming would prevent his being a good sire, although the produce from a mare so bred might have been a great success if she had been mated to a good horse of the Darley Arabian line. His breeding is very similar to the result that might be anticipated from the mating a half-bred horse with a thorough-bred mare; or, to go further, the putting a horse of any inferior blood to a pure Arabian mare—the offspring in both cases *might* prove a great success as far as the individual was concerned, either as a racer or for other purposes, but, if a *horse*, would be of little or no use for the stud.

Although many would say that our racehorse is equally descended from all three lines, and the blood so thoroughly mixed that it cannot be separated, and that it does not matter from which family you select your sire, I consider using a horse either from the Godolphin Arab's or Barb's line, or from the Byerly Turk's, is almost the same as if a Persian, Barb, Turkish, or any other Eastern horse were used in preference to a pure Arabian, which was continually being done in the early history of our stud. There is no warranty for believing the Byerly Turk to have been other than he is described; and of the breeding of the Godolphin Arab or Barb doubts have always been entertained and expressed. The surmise that he was a horse from Northern Africa, and not of pure Arabian blood—and, therefore, far inferior to the Darley Arabian—is, I think, most probably correct, and the history of his line, and the character of his descendants, would confirm this view. The improvement shown in certain individuals of his line by the infusion of other blood on the female side, and yet a failure in these individuals to reproduce this improvement, is quite the criterion of inferior blood on the male side.

The line from the Byerly Turk, as we have seen, was strengthened and supported by frequent and strong infusions of the blood from the Darley Arabian, especially by the sons and daughters of Flying Childers, the most distinguished son of the Darley Arabian; and as the direct line from the last-named horse was not bred back to him for two or three generations by the union of the descendants of his sons and daughters—which is, I think, much to be deplored—had it not been for the Turk's line, the line in direct descent from the Darley Arabian would have been further weakened, but happily they were united in Waxy, and subsequently in many instances. Had daughters of Flying Childers been put to sons of Bartlet's Childers, little or no use need have been made of the Turk's line. The great object ought to have been the confirming of the Darley Arabian's blood. Now that there are so many descendants of his in direct male descent—both horses and mares—it is, I think, well worthy of consideration whether they should not now be almost entirely used for breeding—direct descendants of the Darley Arabian bred among themselves. Were such a system carried out, the descendants of the Godolphin Arab and Barb bred from among themselves, those from the Turk also among themselves, and the Darley Arabian descendants kept to themselves, I believe the Darley Arabian line would live and flourish, and in a few generations the two other lines would become extinct; for the excellence of the first would be found so apparent that the two other lines would be left.

I have been amused from time to time by writings in the papers on the *manufacture* of our racehorse, if the expression may be used. It being generally allowed that although other countries have supplied the blood, not only by the energy and perseverance of the British public, but also by a wonderful amount of science in *crossing*, so well understood in this country, the English racehorse has arrived at his excellence. Some have endeavoured to explain how this has been done by a *judicious* mixture of Turk, Barb, and Arab. The speed and endurance of the Arab being acknowledged, more size was obtained by *judicious* crossings with the Turk and Barb, inferior blood; and, again, whatever coarseness resulted from this infusion from the Barb was *dexterously* kept in abeyance by another cross with the Arab. All this has appeared to me very like the recipes for Christmas plum-puddings—so much of one kind of fruit, so much of another, with a spice of this, that, or the other, cemented or bound together by flour or bread crumbs, which might stand for the former blood of the country before the Eastern importation; but I feel convinced that these 'ingenious' crossings originated from no well-considered system, that all horses of Eastern blood were found to be superior to the old English breed, and little or no distinction made between them, many or most being called or considered as Arabs, although unworthy of the name; and although the immediate good result of the Darley Arabian, as shown by his sons (the only true Arabian so far as we can be certain), alone ought to have convinced us, if other data were wanting (which they are not), of his superiority, no efforts were made to collect more of that pure blood.

At the present time, in spite of the numerous engraftings of inferior strains upon the Darley Arabian line, notwithstanding the loss of the blood in direct male line from his best son, Flying Childers, and the advantage the Turk's line derived from the blood of Flying Childers, the descendants in direct male descent from the Darley Arabian may be unhesitatingly pronounced to keep their heads in front. If any data I have given, or any notes made, may tend to the support of a greater cultivation of this blood, I shall be amply rewarded. It may be said the blood of the three lines may be so intermingled, that even if we were to relinquish the two inferior ones we should never get rid of the blood. Granted, the mischief has been done; we shall no more quite get rid of it than we have of some particles or some of the characteristics of the old native breed; but from breeding from descendants of the Darley Arabian line alone, we might to a very great extent *hold the inferior strains in abeyance.*

Were this tried, and to a certain extent it has—and

many striking examples were shown and alluded to when the line Darley Arabian was under consideration—it would lead to a clearer view of what the results would now have been at this time, if such blood as that of the Darley Arabian had alone been used, and what they would be in a very short time were such pure Arabian blood only to be bred from.

There is one little incidence of breeding that will not have escaped notice—at least I think not—and whenever it has recurred, excellence in that individual, no matter of what family, is noticeable. I allude to the Vauxhall Snap mare and her son Shuttle, he being the produce of a great-great-grandson of the Darley Arabian, through Bartlet's Childers from a mare (the Vauxhall Snap mare), the daughter of a great-great-grandson of the Darley Arabian, through Flying Childers. This breeding, which is nothing more nor less than a union of or breeding back to the Darley Arabian through the two Childers, is seen among others in the pedigree of Sweetmeat, Kingston, Crucifix, Beadsman, Gladiateur, and The Black Doctor. The last-named, although not a distinguished horse at the stud, showed great stoutness and gameness as a racer.

CHAPTER III.

General opinion that impure stock may become pure in eight descents—A different opinion held by the Arabs—Not achieved in the case of the English horse—The breeding of the Eastern horses imported into this country discussed—Remarks on a review of 'Les Races chevalines de la Russie, par J. Mœrder'—Inferences drawn therefrom—Remarks on the horses that followed Flying Childers—Not so purely bred—Great size no proof that degeneracy has not occurred—The English thorough-bred horse not of pure Arabian blood—The excellence of the English horse attributable to Arabian blood—False system of breeding pursued after the time of Childers discussed—Greater results would have been gained if a different system had been pursued—The necessity of obtaining pure stock for the purpose of establishing a standard breed of horses.

In the first chapter it was shown that in the Darley Arabian's time, and just previously to his importation, there really were racers of entirely Eastern blood and origin; but that since the days of his son Flying Childers, no such horses have been bred, but all subsequently have only been partially of Eastern blood, and have inherited many stains of base blood. Had only Eastern blood (instead of pure Arabian) been sufficient to have established a pure race, our horse might have been styled thorough-bred with far more truth then than now.

From the history of the English racer given in the last chapter, it will be seen that the breeding of our horse is very imperfect—that he is not entirely descended from pure blood. It is very commonly considered that, in breeding, any stain that exists may be eradicated in eight generations; that in the eighth descent there is not any difference to be detected in form and appearance between the newly formed breed and the pure parent stock. In other words, the pure blood infused into the impure or inferior stock will have washed away and obliterated all stains and flaws in eight descents. There are others, however, who hold a different opinion; among those the Arabs. 'It is impossible,' says the Emir Abd-el-Kader, 'we think, to get a pure race out of a stock the blood of which is impure.' On the other hand, it is a well-authenticated fact, it is quite possible to restore to its primitive nobleness a breed that has become impoverished, but without any *taint* in its blood. In a word, a race may be restored, the degeneracy of which has not been occasioned by any admixture of blood.

But allowing the opinion to be correct, that in eight descents impure blood may be obliterated, to arrive at the desired result it is necessary, in each and every descent anterior to the ninth, to return on the male side to the original pure blood. Now, certainly, as shown in Chapter II., our horse, since the days of Flying Childers, has not been so bred. I fail to trace any systematic return to Arabian blood for the prescribed period of eight generations; or, indeed, a return to horses of only Eastern blood. On the contrary, horses and mares only partially descended from Eastern horses have been bred from.

But, after all, this system of breeding—namely, that of

trying to eradicate base blood and defects by the engrafting of pure blood on the male side for eight descents, is a very unsafe one to rest upon. Its being open to question is unsatisfactory; it is opposed in principle to the experience of the Arabs, the most renowned horse breeders in the world; contrary to their practice, and, so far as I see, has nothing to recommend it.

Should the desired result be attained even in the eighth generation, and there should not be any *appreciable* difference from the original pure stock, it is quite possible that the eighth descent might not be capable of handing down to posterity through succeeding generations the primal characteristics of its originator. It is far more probable that in each succeeding generation, after the infusion of the pure blood on the male side had ceased, the attributes so derived would grow fainter and fainter. The greatest test of pure breeding is stoutness and endurance, combined with a high degree of speed.

'Look in a horse' (says Abd-el-Kader) 'for speed and bottom; one that has speed alone, and no bottom, must have a blemish in his descent; and one that has bottom alone, and no speed, must have some defect—open or concealed.'

It is often asserted, and very generally allowed, that our thoroughbred has deteriorated and become degenerate, and some have urged this degeneracy has taken place from the system of early training which has been pursued, rather than from any fault or deficiency in the breeding of our horses.

What is put forward in this country as a plea for the deterioration, degeneracy, and want of endurance of our *thorough*-bred horse, is considered by the Arabs absolutely necessary to the development of the inherent good qualities of their horse. General Daumas was informed by Abd-el-Kader that in the Sahara the pure-bred descendant of the Arabian is taught to lead when a foal; when it has entered on its second year (a yearling, in fact), it is ridden a mile or two, or even sixteen; and after it has completed eighteen months they do not fear to fatigue it. The Emir also states that unless a horse has been broken from a foal, he will never be able to perform the great feats and long journeys for which the Arabian is justly famed. Should his education be put off until he is four years old, he is almost worthless; Abd-el-Kader would decline to buy such a horse. This is his experience after having seen upwards of 10,000 colts reared. He also affirms, when he has made long and rapid marches at the head of 12,000 or 15,000 horsemen, horses, however lean, if they had been early broken into fatigue, never fell out of the ranks. The same system is pursued by the Arabs in the East—early training and hard work is the rule. M. Pétiniaud, who wandered among the Arab tribes from Diarbekir and Aleppo in the north, to the confines of Nejed in the south, thus writes to General Daumas: 'I have witnessed in Asia what you have written of in Africa.'

In an article (I think in 'The Times') some few years ago, I noticed the following: 'Although the staying qualities of our racehorses are certainly on the decrease, and although aged running horses and mares have disappeared from our racecourses, it is certain that the racing yearlings annually offered under the hammer are, on the average, growing larger and stronger.' May it not be inferred from this—Firstly, that size is not the great or ultimate desideratum ; and secondly, that the strength this size would seem to indicate is fallacious, and not real ? And is not the cause of the degeneracy and deterioration to be accounted for by the fact that our horse is not *thorough-bred*—not bred completely from a pure and original race ? And is not this the secret of our horse being less enduring and less lasting than the Arabian ? Stoutness and endurance, combined with speed, contained in a beautiful form of perfect symmetry, being the attributes, characteristics, and very birth-right of a pure and noble race, are not to be *invariably* reproduced by a breed of less pure blood, nor by a crossed and inferior breed.

It would be well to take a retrospect of the Arabian and other Eastern horses which have been brought over to this country. They have been styled Arabians, Turks, Barbs, Persians, Egyptian, Toorkoman, and foreign horses.

The value of the blood of these imported horses would be greater or less in proportion as they may be regarded as being wholly, or only partially, of Arabian blood. In looking at the Turks generally, it is to be considered, were they merely horses of the Turkish dominions—the descendants, doubtless, of breeds improved by the Arabian—or were they really Arab horses imported into

Turkey? Now it is a well-known fact, that with the exception of an occasional present, either to the Sultan at Constantinople, or to the Pasha of Egypt, there are no good Arabs either in Turkey or Egypt; and the dislike Arabs have towards the Turks would prevent more being sent than absolute policy might dictate, and they would not willingly supply them with horses. Even at a very recent period it is most probable that there was but one real Arabian in the Sultan's possession, and that had been obtained from an Englishman; and the far more reasonable supposition is that the horses brought to this country from Turkey were only partly of Arabian blood. And in many parts of Asia Minor are some very useful breeds of horses which have been improved by the Arabian, with excellent legs and feet—apparently in that respect everything to be desired; but they have not the rare combination of qualities as in the Arabian, nor his springiness and flexibility. Yet, without doubt, many of these have been reckoned as Arabs in England.

With respect to the horses imported under the name of Barbs, it must be remembered that, although the Emir Abd-el-Kader says the '*horses of the Sahara*' are the pure descendants of Arabians, he also says all *Barbs* are not of unmixed blood, but that the breed has not been kept pure, and has degenerated, and especially towards the coast. And General Daumas, who has given the subject the greatest attention, says: 'We may rest assured that, for the most part, the animals sold to us' (he is referring to Barbs) 'are of an inferior order.' Of the horses styled Arabian little or nothing is now known of them or their antecedents, if they were ever ascertained (but Bloody-Buttocks and the Leedes Arabian would appear to have been excellent horses—especially the latter), with the single exception of the Darley Arabian, whose history is known, and his family was mentioned, in the account of the line he founded, in a former chapter. And as further reference will be made to that hereafter, I will only add, his memory is still retained among the Arabs; and I have been informed, horses descended direct from him are still to be met with in Arabia.

From a review which appeared in 'Bell's Life' a year or two ago on a work entitled, 'Aperçu historique sur les Institutions hippiques et les Races chevalines de la Russie, par J. Mœrder,' St. Petersburg, 1868, inferences may be drawn as to the types of horses past and present, which support the often asserted opinion of the deterioration of the English thorough-bred horse. It was remarked: 'It will be flattering to our countrymen to read the following amongst other observations: "Nous allons maintenant passer à l'examen des types de chevaux de haras. La première place est occupée par le pur sang arabe et le cheval de course anglais. Ces deux types servent à la formation de toutes nos meilleures espèces."' And again, when speaking farther on of the purity of the blood of English horses, M. Mœrder states: 'Le cheval anglais, dans sa forme primitive, était remarquable par sa haute taille, sa belle tête, qu'il tenait du cheval arabe; ses petites oreilles, son cou long et gracieux, son dos court, sa croupe haute et droite, sa queue bien adaptée, ses jambes fortes et bien formées, son allure ferme.' These quotations appear to be very significant.

It might be sufficiently flattering to the Arabs, if they cared about other people's concerns, to know that the Arabian horse had given such excellent points to ours, as we find by the above description he *formerly* possessed; but we can hardly have cause to congratulate ourselves, when we compare our 'cheval de course' of the present day with the animal M. Mœrder shows him to have been 'dans sa forme primitive.' Formerly he was distinguished by his fine carriage, by his beautiful head, of the Arabian type, his small ears, his short back, his long and elegant neck ('gracieux' well expresses it), his high and straight croup, his well set-on tail, his strong and well-formed limbs, and his good true action.

All these are eminently the attributes of the Arabian, and, according to M. Mœrder, were to be seen originally or formerly (in a modified degree, I think must be understood) in the breed of horses derived from him, which we call thorough-bred. Do we see all these points, as a rule, in the modern racer? Are they the invariable or prevailing characteristics? The answer must be in the negative. The grand carriage of the Arabian is not seen; the head is very often quite the reverse of the Arabian's; he has often long and large ears instead of small ones; his neck, though sometimes long, is as often short, and very seldom 'gracieux'; his back has certainly become elongated. Alas! what shall we say when we come to the high quarter, such as is seen among Arabians. Ours is but very drooping. Instead of the well set-on tail, he has often one set on rather low, and but seldom *carried*; and instead of well-formed limbs, do we not too often find badly-shaped and weak legs? His action is not always good all round, nor is his gait always bold and steady.

There is certainly a considerable alteration in the structure of our horse from his Arabian ancestor. He may be classed as more like the Toorkoman or Persian horse, or the Barb. It is my belief there has been some change in the last thirty years. His shoulders are not generally so well thrown back, nor so long, nor so powerful, his quarters more drooping. This alteration of form gives a longer back and barrel, and perhaps a greater *appearance* of length, but it is not real: the structure is altered for the worse; the various parts are not so well placed to act with the greatest advantage, and it is contrary to the form of his Arabian ancestor. It is no unfrequent thing to see short, jumped-up, long-legged horses stripped on the course. Many are coarse, others are weedy, some both coarse and weedy, and others positively ugly. If you can notice a horse's back as being long, either his shoulders or his quarters, or both, are faulty: too long a back with good quarters is a sure sign of upright shoulders; if the shoulders are well placed, but accompanied by a long back, the quarters are short, or have a wrong direction; or it may be that a horse with too long a back may have upright shoulders and short quarters.

I think any one who has examined and does study attentively our blood stock will allow these changes and modifications do exist in our modern racer, and that no unfaithful picture has been drawn. The modern racer does not show the fine points and attributes which were formerly seen in horses of an older date, imprinted upon them by their Arabian ancestry. In other words, the English thorough-bred horse has failed to hand down to his descendants the primal characteristics of the pure Arabian, or, indeed, retained the modified points which were observable formerly. Can this be flattering to our countrymen? Now the question will naturally arise, Why have not these points been preserved and perpetuated? Is it not owing to one grand cause, or—to speak, perhaps, more correctly—accounted for by one simple fact, he is not really thoroughbred; he is not of pure race?

In going through the pedigrees of the modern horses whose history has been sketched in the second chapter, reference should be made to the three tables of pedigrees which have been fully drawn out, and it will be seen that every individual inherits the flaws which are shown to have existed in Matchem, Eclipse, and Herod, and, in addition, the multiplication of these deficiencies; for, although good blood is accumulated in certain horses, by the in-breeding to certain families containing the blood of the Darley Arabian, inasmuch as his blood has only descended to modern horses (even in direct descent) through half-bred horses, with the accumulation of good strains, the number of stains which were in the pedigrees of these half-bred ancestors has also increased. If this be the case with the best and more carefully bred among our horses, what can be said of those of much mixed pedigrees, where stains are as numerous, but derived, perhaps, through inferior horses, and without the advantage of the *concentration* of good blood? In the case of our breed called through-bred, besides the impure strains which are still handed down, fresh stains may be said to appear. Mares in the Stud Book have produced foals to half-bred horses (I have known an instance where a cart-horse was used). Some of these mares have since produced animals which have been successful. These horses, used at the stud, hand down the stain immediately derived from their dam, in addition to former ones. Again, some horses that have appeared on the Turf as half-breed are now in the Stud Book.

Lath, the first son of the Godolphin Arab or Barb, own brother to Cade, their dam being Roxana, was considered the best horse that had been at Newmarket since Flying Childers. It must be remembered he made his appearance in the days of degeneracy that happened after the time of Childers, and was therefore opposed to inferior horses, the offspring of half-bred sires and dams; but, although he was considered a wonder, it is recorded that Lath did not come up to the standard or the excellence of Childers. Those who had seen Childers were able to appreciate the difference, although the young sportsmen may have been satisfied.

So, again, Eclipse, a descendant in male line from the Darley Arabian, and on the side of his dam from the Godolphin Arab, was deemed a phenomenon. Why was this? A little reflection on the sketch of the history of our horse will explain it. From the time of Flying Childers the horse was retrograding—by Eastern blood having been set aside in favour of crossed-bred horses. The result became apparent; a deficiency in every respect was discernible. It is clearly to be seen that our horse then did not possess the high qualities of Flying Childers and the horses of his time or immediately before him, many of whom were entirely of Eastern blood. But in Eclipse there was another fresh infusion of Eastern blood—Spiletta, his dam, being the grand-daughter of an Eastern horse. It was a happy circumstance; it answered. Her sire, Regulus, *son* of the Godolphin Arab, distinguished himself among the degenerated horses of that period; but he himself was not of Eastern blood alone; and on both sides of Eclipse's pedigree, although there was a re-union of Eastern and Arab blood, there *were many stains.* But because Eclipse was superior to the two generations before him, and to the horses of his time, it is no proof that he was at all equal to the racers which were entirely of Eastern blood at the period of the Darley Arabian. And at the present time there is nothing to guide us to the belief that the racer of our day has improved upon the form of Flying Childers, but many things, and especially the fact that he is not now of such pure breeding, to lead us to the conviction that he is inferior. What have we to guide us to the assumption that our present horse is superior, even to Eclipse? Certainly not the distances that are now run, nor the weights now carried, against those under which former distances were accomplished.

I am not one of those always lamenting over our horse's degeneracy, although I may be quite willing to accept the convictions which those who can look further back are compelled to admit; but I maintain our horse is not so good as he might be if we had pursued a different and more careful style of breeding. Those who argue that the horse has not deteriorated point to certain stallions of a large size, and, although they as a rule ignore the time test, yet they refer you to the time in which certain great races have been run, as being faster during the last few years than a short period before. This latter—if a correct test—could only show that there had been an improvement in the last thirty years or half-century. But even this is a delusion; for I have it on very good authority that hardly any races for several years past have been truly timed, the horses having started seconds before the time-keepers begin to take time.

Time, if properly taken, and races be truly run, must be a tolerably correct test, and be valuable as a guide to those who come after us; but if time be not taken, fifty years hence people will imagine that we had *stayers*, from the fact that there were some races of two and three miles, and, having no time to guide them, will presume they were run from end to end.

Does experience teach us that 'those fine-sized, big-boned thorough-breds,' which are sometimes seen, and brought forward as an emphatic proof that there is no necessity, at any rate, for the breed of horses to deteriorate, are as a rule the stoutest, the truest, and most enduring, or that as stallions they are the sires which beget the stoutest stock? Is not the contrary rather the rule? The history of the thoroughbred, and more especially the tables of pedigrees given at the end, most conclusively prove our horse is neither altogether of Arabian blood, nor yet even entirely of Eastern extraction, and therefore certainly not thorough-bred. Moreover, the three horses, Herod, Matchem, and Eclipse, from which all modern horses are descended, were nothing more than half-bred, got by half-bred sires from half-bred dams; which completely destroys the theory that the English racer is entirely of Arabian blood—'the true son of Arabia Deserta.'

'As thorough-bred as Eclipse' is a common expression in speaking of a horse's claim to pure breeding. If he be not better bred than Eclipse, he is but a cocktail. People are apt to talk of horses tracing back to Eclipse and Herod, and in looking at pedigrees which are seldom drawn out so far as either; but by seeing a combination of the blood of Herod and Eclipse, say, 'There's blood for you; good enough for anything!' Kind reader, look carefully at the pedigrees of your favourite horses; the real interest and the very essence of which only begin with those up to which you are content to trace. Look, and find that the 'terribly high-bred cattle,' which you fondly imagine to be without peer, are the descendants of a half-bred horse and a half-bred dam. Look a little further back, to the days of Queen Anne, and trace the pedigrees also given of some horses of her days, in which, at all events, nothing but Eastern blood can be found;

and what becomes of the thoroughbred of modern days?

Those who assert that our horse's excellence is owing to our consummate skill in breeding rather than to procuration of original stock of good description (the Eastern stock), and which was supported by Mr. William Percivall in his address at the University College in 1834, seem to be forgetful of the fact that it was immediately after the introduction of Eastern blood, not before, that the English became celebrated for their horses. Youatt, who quotes Mr. Percivall, says, 'and although, perhaps on the whole, the English were not far behind their continental neighbours, yet at no period until within the last century and a half has Great Britian been at all distinguished on this account'—that is, the excellence of its horses. Youatt made the remark in 1850; so the century and a half from that date takes us back not only to when Eastern blood had been acknowledged as superior, and had wrought great changes in our native breed, but to the very days of the Leedes and Darley Arabians, when there were actually horses and mares of entirely Eastern blood; and only just before Flying Childers, in whose days our horse arrived at the zenith of his excellence. The fallacy of such an assertion can hardly fail to be apparent. Common sense, let alone consummate judgment and skill in breeding, ought to have dictated the advisability of perpetuating such blood as Flying Childers' and other horses also of entirely Eastern blood, and principally of Arabian, instead of allowing it to become degenerate by resorting to mares of common blood, and afterwards breeding from half-bred horses and mares. Consummate skill devoted to breeding, if it had been applied to drawing out the excellences of the best stock, must have achieved a higher success and greater results than has resulted from the continued system of breeding from a mixed and half-bred stock. As Eastern blood had been found more than 200 years ago necessary for horses of any degree of excellence, and of all Eastern blood the Arabian is incomparable, even if no more skill and no greater perception and ability than have been displayed in breeding from half-bred stock, had been devoted to the incomparable Arabian blood, must not the results have been far greater than at present? Even if we allow the horse to have improved upon the form of Eclipse, being now, as in the days of Eclipse, but a half-bred animal, he cannot be compared to Flying Childers, altogether of Eastern blood, and two-thirds Arabian. I must crave indulgence for using the plainest language, and for repeatedly urging the fact of our horse being only half-bred since the days of Childers, which is supported by proof from our Stud Book. What would be thought of a proposal to breed *thorough-bred horses* (racers) from what are called half-bred horses and mares now-a-days? But it is the very thing we have been doing for the last 150 years; it is the very thing we are doing now at this very time!

Those who may have no knowledge of the history of our horse, may gather some information on the subject by following me so far, and cannot fail to see he is not completely bred, nor entirely bred from the best blood, nor completely bred from a pure and original race.

Nearly a century after the birth of Flying Childers, Fair Ellen is born to an Eastern horse styled the Wellesley Grey Arabian. She was the dam of Lilias, winner of the Oaks, 1826, and of The Exquisite, who ran second for the Derby, 1829; and of Euryone, granddam of Safeguard, a horse of very considerable merit. Unfortunately his blindness (derived doubtless from his sire Defence) always prevented his employment with valuable mares, coupled also with the prejudice against modern Arabian blood; but his soundness in every other respect, the extraordinary goodness of his feet and legs, and his wonderful constitution, and his success as a sire, considering the inferior mares put to him, have been noticed and recorded by 'Stonehenge.' Slight as was the infusion of Eastern blood, it was not without beneficial results. Perhaps, with the exception of the Darley Arabian, no better Arabs have appeared in this country than the black and bay Arabians presented by Imaun Seyéed, of Muscat, to his Majesty William IV., but I believe they were never used as sires with thorough-bred mares, nor with an Arabian mare also sent with them; and so the opportunity of trying Arabian blood was again *lost* or thrown away. These horses, doubtless, came from Nejed. The Arabian horse is not indigenous to Oman.

Assuming that purity of blood is necessary for the attainment of the full amount of excellence in the horse, it is obvious, for the purpose of founding a standard breed in this or any other country, in which the horse did not exist in a pure or perfect state, that stock of pure blood should have been, and also should now be, obtained for such a purpose, instead of having, in the first instance, engrafted a few individuals of more or less pure blood, and that chiefly on the male side, on to the former heterogeneous stock, as in this country, and then subsequently breeding entirely from their half-bred descendants.

The horse of such a character, to found a race of true thorough-bred horses, and in which alone such requisite perfections can be found, will be discussed in the second part.

PART 2

THE ARABIAN HORSE.

CHAPTER I.

THE ORIGIN AND ANTIQUITY OF THE ARABIAN.

Different opinions as to his origin—Probable early history discussed—Views against his being originally located in Arabia — Objections answered—No lack of horses in Arabia during the time of Mohammed—Held in great estimation very shortly after his death—The horse taken into Africa at an early date—Indication of the horse being in Arabia before he is mentioned as being in Egypt—Times and country of Job discussed—The horse always ridden in Arabia—The unchanging character of the Arabs, the probable means of the horse having been kept in a pure state—The horse created good : the original not improved upon—The Persian horse probably owed his improvement to Arab blood—Short dissertation on Jonadab : his occupation—The Rechabites, Midianites, and Ishmaelites—The horse likely to become degenerate in Egypt.

The silver Arab with his purple veins,
The true blood royal of his race.—*Yule.*

AS to the origin and antiquity of the Arabian different opinions exist. Some imagine the Arabian horse to be an improved specimen of the species, bred up from the original race, which has been presumed was of a very poor and sorry description, and only of comparatively recent date a native of Arabia; others believe him to have been originally located and domesticated in Arabia. I may say at once I entertain the latter opinion, and believe him to be the sole pure representative of the species.

I will give a short sketch of his probable early history, and then bring forward such matter as may bear upon the subject, in proof and support.

When the horse made his exit from the Ark with the other animals saved alive from the Flood, B.C. 2349-48, I do not mean to insist he immediately made his way into Central Arabia, and was found there by those who first inhabited that country, although such a supposition is very far from improbable. The same law of nature that dictates to him and every animal what is best for them—the fine instinct which he has received from his Creator, and which enables him to find his nearest way home, or if cast adrift at sea, at once to turn his head to the nearest land, might as easily have directed him to Arabia, the soil and climate of which are peculiarly adapted to him and the retention of his primal characteristics.

It may be supposed rather, that he would follow the saved inhabitants of the world, or be taken by them to the plains of Shinar; and when, rather more than a hundred years after the Flood—during which time he would have increased and multiplied—the Tower of Babel being in course of erection, the work was suddenly stopped by the confusion of tongues, and the families of Noah dispersed to seek localities for themselves, that he would be settled and domesticated with some of these families.

When Nimrod was founding Babylon he may have retained some for his future kingdom; and Misraim may have carried the horse into Egypt; and why not with equal probability that family which went into Central Arabia, and first peopled it? Why should the horse be denied to that country, the most propitious to him, and where, at the present time, he is found in the purest form, to a people of the highest antiquity?

Eber, the great-grandson of Shem, had two sons, Joktan (or Kahtan as spelt in Arabia) and Peleg; the latter, the founder of Abraham's family, and subsequently through Abraham's son Ishmael became joined with the descendants of Joktan. 'In the days of Peleg the earth was divided,' or, as I understand, the dispersion took place at Babel. Joktan and his family went down into Central Arabia, about the time Nimrod was founding Babylon, or perhaps before. They must have been, as their descendants are now, horse-fanciers. The horse was ridden in Arabia; he was not put to degrading work; he was a hunter and a war horse. The horse was ridden only in Arabia, not used for harness, as subsequently by other nations. Joktan and his family were settled in that part of Arabia even now called Kahtan, and to whose inhabitants the term Ketanic is still applied, reaching from near Mecca in the west to Jebel Toweek in the east.

It was from this district, in all probability, that the descendants of Joktan, if not at war among themselves, made frequent raids upon their northern neighbours; and among them the Sabæans, mounted upon their matchless coursers, performed a true Arab feat, making a swoop upon Job's peaceful possessions, carrying off his cattle, and killing his servants with the edge of the sword. When war was not the order of the day, the chase occupied their time, either for pastime or in quest of food, and when the ostrich was the game, to try the speed and endurance of their horses. Thus would pass many generations; but at an early period the horse was taken from Arabia into Africa, and founded the breed known as the horses of Sahara. Since, both before and after the time of Mohammed, importations of Arabian horses into Africa have taken place.

At a later period the Arabian horse became more generally known, and played a very conspicuous part. When, after the death of Mohammed, Arabia had become the centre of an empire second to none in extent, he was taken out into all lands, east, north, and west—into Europe, Africa, and other parts of Asia, and left his mark upon the degenerated and changed breeds of other countries through which he passed; and at this day, according to the amount of Arab blood to be found in the modern horse, in any part of the world, is he valuable.

Scripture tells us that Joktan had thirteen sons, one of whom was named Sheba, 'and their dwelling was from Mesha, as thou goest unto Sephar, a mount of the East.'

Mecca in the Hejaz, allowed to be one of the most

ancient cities, is supposed to be identical with the Mesha of Scripture (of this there can be little doubt), but some have objected to Central Arabia as being the territory occupied by Joktan, as they know of no 'mount' in the East. A glance at the map appended to Mr. Palgrave's book of travel through Central Arabia will dispel such doubts at once.

It will be seen that between Mecca and Jebel Toweek—which latter is, strictly speaking, Nejed Proper—lies the district called Kahtan. Jebel Toweek literally means, we are told, a little twist or garland of mountains, which would answer to the description 'a mount of the East.' At the foot of the collection of little mounts, at the northern extremity, but still east from Mecca, is a town now called Zulphar, which, I think, might well be the Sephar of Scripture, the western boundary of Joktan's dominion. From profane history we learn that Joktan, the father of the ancient Arabs, had thirty-one sons, and that he first wore the diadem in Yemen. He was succeeded by Yarab, Yarab by his son Yashab, and Yashab by Abd-Shems, who was a great and successful monarch. He built the city of Saba, and formed vast reservoirs above the city to supply the inhabitants and surrounding lands with water. Abd-Shems was succeeded by his son Hamyar, so called from his wearing red clothes, and he gave his name to a tribe. He was succeeded by a line of seventeen kings, from one of whom, named Africus, the continent of Africa derived its name. It is believed the Queen of Sheba followed this line of seventeen kings.

Another son of Joktan founded the kingdom of Hejaz. Whether Joktan first settled in the district known as Kahtan, and afterwards founded the kingdom of Yemen, or whether the kingdoms of Yemen and Hejaz were first established, and his descendants afterwards spread themselves over Kahtan, is not of much consequence; but that such was their territory, and identical with that as described from Mesha to Sephar, a mount of the East, there can be but little doubt. In this country, then, the horse was established not later than about one hundred years after the Deluge; it may have been simultaneously with other families, who might have taken horses with them. Here only the horse would appear to have been kept in a pure and unmixed state, and to have been preserved from degeneration, as, after a lapse of four thousand years, we find him still in the purest and noblest form, unchanged and unchanging, in pristine beauty, and in the hands of a people the most ancient and least affected by the outward world; if indeed he did not find his way there immediately after the exodus from the Ark, which is by no means improbable, and which will now be considered.

Although there are reasons for believing that the horse was distributed over many parts of the world before the Deluge, it is only consistent to believe that the most perfect specimens of all things living were taken into the Ark. Where this was built cannot be stated; but we know that when the waters subsided it rested upon the mountains of Ararat, which, however, is no evidence that it was constructed there—all probability would point to a less elevated locality. The wisdom of the exit taking place from such a lofty position is at once apparent when we consider for one moment in what a state the lowlands must have been after having been deluged for so long a time. What situation could be more admirably chosen, both with regard to its central position for the replenishing of the earth, and also on account of the health of the long-imprisoned inhabitants, than a mountain land and its surrounding slopes! Even if we knew the exact spot where the Ark was constructed, it would not necessarily indicate the original locality of the horse; nor is it necessary to believe that Noah, in compliance with the Divine command, took unto him any animals that might be immediately around him, or that the selection was left to him. Taking into consideration the antagonistic character and habits of many of the creatures, both small and great, it is very easy to believe that those intended for preservation, 'to keep seed alive upon the face of all the earth,' would be drawn together by the Divine Power and Infinite Wisdom—many specimens perhaps from great distances; and if that part of the world now known as Arabia were then, as Gibbon says it is now, the most propitious to the horse, that from thence came the horses to the Ark. That they were divinely directed, and not selected by Noah, is borne out by Holy Scripture. In Genesis, ch. vi. verse 20, Noah is told 'two of every sort shall come *unto* thee to keep them alive.' In ch. vii. verse 1, he is directed to enter the Ark with his house. At verse 7 it is stated, 'Noah went in, and his sons, and his wife, and his sons' wives with him into the Ark'; verses 8 and 9 narrate how that two and two of all flesh (the male and the female) went *unto* Noah into the Ark. It is also repeated in verse 15 that they *went* in *unto* Noah into the Ark two and two of all flesh; and in verse 16 it is stated, 'and the Lord shut him in.'

Noah, on the appointed day, went into the Ark with his family. Then entered unto him two and two of all creatures, and, when all were in, the door was shut. Following this train of thought, it would not require any great stretch of imagination to believe that the horses, freed from their long confinement, upon leaving the Ark would at once, or so soon as the state of the ground would permit, seek the place from whence they had come, and which was most congenial to them.

If this supposition be correct—and I confess I have a decided opinion in its favour—the horse would be found in Arabia by Joktan and his family after the dispersion at Babel, who would hold him in their complete possession; and from Arabia the horse would have gone forth into other parts of the world (as he has subsequently done at different periods of his history), and this would allow ample time for the horse to be established in Egypt by the time he is first mentioned in the days of Joseph.

There is yet another view. Bishop Patrick, in his Notes on Genesis, believes that all the posterity of Noah, much less Noah himself, were not at the building of Babel; and therefore the language of Noah was not changed. It is probable, also, although I would not insist upon this view, that Shem and his descendants, through one family of whom all nations are blessed, were separate from those who were at Babel; and as Eber, the great-grandson of Shem, was the father of two great families—the Hebrews and the ancient Arabians—it is possible that, as to the former family was confided the care of the knowledge of the true and only God, so might the charge of man's most valued servant be committed to the other family. I speak this with all reverence. That the language of Shem's family, or a considerable portion of it, was not changed or confounded, is probable, from the fact that the language of his descendants, the Hebrews and Arabians, is very similar, even at the present day. Of course the language of Ishmael was identical with Abraham's, and, being the same, or nearly so, with the descendants of Joktan, which had probably become only slightly modified by time, was one of the reasons which rendered his fusion with the ancient Arabians the more easy.

Against the views I hold, it has constantly been urged as a proof that Egypt is the original country of the horse, that the first direct mention of the horse in Scripture is of his being in that country. This cannot, I think, be taken as a proof that Egypt was the original country of the horse after the Flood, or that the horse was not in Arabia before the time when he is first mentioned in Scripture. If so, it would show that the horse was not in any other part of the world, and that he was first known and heard of some time between Abraham's visit to Egypt and Joseph's sojourn there. The Scriptures do not give the history of animals, although much valuable information on such a subject may be gained from them. The horse is only mentioned when he performs a part in any event in the country that may enter into Biblical history; he is first mentioned when Joseph gave the starving inhabitants of Egypt, during the seven years of famine, bread in exchange for *horses* and for the flocks, &c. This was centuries after the Flood. When Abram went down into Egypt, no mention is made of the horse: he is not among the gifts presented to the patriarch; and so, equally, it might be argued that at that time the horse was unknown in Egypt, although probably it was because such a gift would not have been acceptable. When Joseph goes up into Canaan to bury his father, as the horse takes a part in the procession, he is again mentioned. A writer in Blaine's 'Rural Sports' says, 'It appears difficult to reconcile the plentitude of horses in Arabia with the Scriptural account that when Saul, who became king of Israel, B.C. 1095, made a successful war against this very country, his plunder consisted of camels, sheep, oxen, and asses only; no mention being made of horses.' And Youatt 'On the Horse' states that so late as the seventh century the Arabs had few horses, and those of little value; for when Mohammed attacked the Koreish near Mecca, he had but two horses in his whole army. And at the close of his murderous campaign, although he drove off 24,000 camels, 140,000 sheep, and carried away 24,000 oz. of silver, not one horse appears in the list of plunder.

But another writer in Blaine's 'Rural Sports,' Mr. Burchett, of Truro, says Arabia possessed horses in great numbers at a very early period of the world, and has stronger claims to be entitled the primal seat of these animals than any other country. His opinion is partly grounded upon the extreme antiquity of the Arabs, whom he regards as the most ancient people in the world. Gibbon also gives Arabia the credit of being the genuine and original country of the horse. 'It is a climate the most propitious, not indeed to *size*, but to the *spirit* of that generous animal.' Niebuhr says, 'Some animals appear to be originally natives of Arabia, for they are not common through other regions of the East; they retain their *primary* instincts in a higher perfection, and are more eminently distinguished by strength and beauty here than elsewhere; such are the horse, the ass, and the camel.' And Mr. Gifford Palgrave says the kingdom of Oman is as celebrated for camels as Central Arabia for its horses.

One would not be far wrong in assigning the ass to the more northern districts; the camel to the south-eastern, and the horses to Central Arabia.

With reference to the remark that horses were not part of the plunder taken by King Saul from the Amalekites, it must be borne in mind that that people, the descendants of one of the sons of Esau, of far less antiquity than the Ketanie Arabs or the Ishmaelites, occupied a very small portion of Arabia, that small peninsula between the gulfs of Akabah and Zuez, a district not adapted to the rearing of horses, even if the Amalekites were possessed of them. But because he was not found among that people, is no proof he was not in Arabia; nor, again, the fact that afterwards King Solomon got his horses from Egypt, and gold and silver from Arabia; the gold and silver would be brought, no doubt, from the south of Yemen and Hadramaut by ships up the Red Sea, manned by King Hiram's sailors, and landed at Elath, King Solomon's seaport, on the Gulf of Akabah.

His communication with Egypt was easy, the distance not very great, and he had constant and intimate intercourse with Egypt. Horses and chariots could be brought up very easily from thence; there would appear to have been a regular trade; the prices are fixed—a chariot at six hundred shekels of silver, and a horse at one hundred and fifty. And through King Solomon's interest, the kings of the Hittites and of Syria also obtained them; so horses were not general at that time in Syria. These horses reared in the fat lands of Rameses, whether they were the descendants of the horses from Arabia, or of those that Misraim may have taken, would by this time have lost much of their pristine beauty and perfection, and have become grosser, coarser, of a more bulky body, and more suitable for dragging chariots.

But Solomon had other horses. In 1 Kings, chap. x. verse 25, we read, after being told that all the earth sought Solomon, 'and they brought every man his present, vessels of silver and vessels of gold, and garments, and armour, and spices, *horses* and mules, a rate year by year.' It is quite likely the Arabs deemed it expedient, if not absolutely necessary, to present horses to King Solomon from time to time as gifts, even if not as tribute, and they would do this far more readily than they do now to the Sultan at Constantinople or the Viceroy in Egypt, for they looked upon Solomon as a kinsman, but they detest the Turks and despise them as aliens.

The statement alluded to just before, that, so late as the seventh century, the Arabs had few horses, and those of little value, is not supported by history, and would appear to be based upon the absence of the horses among the things plundered. This is very easily explained. Mohammed had a very up-hill game to fight. During his early career he was badly off for horses, and he could not possibly capture them. When successful in action, or plundering caravans, he took much plunder; but, without cavalry, how could he capture *Arab horsemen?* But some he had at command. It is commonly reported, he and his five followers fled from Mecca to Medina on horses. The Arabs say he had only one follower, and he went on a camel. But in the second year of the Hegira, we read that Mohammed sent out on one occasion a body of thirty horse to attack a rich caravan going to Mecca; on another, in the same year, a body of sixty or eighty horse.

It was at the battle of Ohod, in the third year of the Hegira, that Mohammed is said to have had only two horses with him. But that is no proof that there were no horses in Arabia. For the Koreish met him with a force of 800 men, 200 of whom were horsemen. Mohammed suffered defeat by a charge of cavalry commanded by Caled Ebn-el-Wallid. Mohammed at this time was continually employed in plundering caravans. When he lost the battle of Ohod, what horse he had (a considerable force, 500 horse) was away on a plundering expedition under his follower Zeid, who came down upon a very rich caravan at Al-Karda in Nejed. The booty taken on this occasion was estimated at 25,000 dahrems or pieces of silver.

On another occasion, after having been compelled to raise the siege of the castle of El-Tayef, into which Malec the chief and his fighting-men had thrown themselves, Mohammed took the town of Waha, in which Malec had caused to be deposited many of their most valuable effects, which is said to have consisted of 24,000 camels, 40,000 sheep, and 4,000 oz. of silver, in addition to 6,000 captives. If Malec were possessed of horses—which most probably he was—and they not away from home on any expedition, they would be with his fighting-men, and form part of the garrison of El-Tayef, and which did *not* succumb to Mohammed.

Mohammed was not slow in learning the full value of the horse, and during his early career doubtless often deplored his own deficiency in cavalry. Having seen how essential the horse was to rapid movement, either in the advance to attack, or for security in case of defeat, he was loud in the praise of that generous animal, and left maxims regarding his care and treatment to his followers.

It was in the ninth year of the Hegira—only one year before the death of Mohammed—that the greater number of Arabian tribes sent embassies to him, tendering their submission, or, rather, making alliances, as many of them did so to suit their own convenience, and did not really believe in him as a prophet. They had been watching with interest the results of his protracted war and disputes with the Koreish.

Again, during the reign of Omar, the second Caliph, Abu Obeidah, his commander-in-chief, after the battle of Yermouk—which decided the fate of Syria—in the division of the spoil, made a distinction between horse and foot, and between those who were mounted on Arabian horses and those who rode horses of a *foreign* breed. All cavalry in general had three times the value in spoils to what the infantry had; but the owner of a *true Arabian* horse had a double portion to what the master of any other horse had. This was in the fifteenth year of the Hegira, very shortly after the death of Mohammed, and it proves that Arabian horses were neither scarce nor of little value in the sixth and the beginning of the seventh centuries. If there had been only a few horses in Arabia, and those of no value, in Mohammed's time, it would have been impossible, in so short a period as fifteen years, to have established a breed of such great value and well-acknowledged superiority as the *true Arabian horse.*

Moreover, Abd-el-Kader, the celebrated Emir in Africa, has stated that the Arabian horse was taken into Africa anterior to Islam by two Herimetic tribes, that the horses of the Sahara are their pure descendants, and that the first family or race among them is the Hamyan. It has been shown that Hamyar, who gave his name to a tribe, was the sixth only in descent from Joktan, and that among the seventeen kings who succeeded him was one Africus, who called Africa after himself. Perhaps in the time of Hamyar the Arabian horse was taken into Africa; hardly later than that of Africus.

Here it may not be out of place to draw attention to collateral events. When Abram went down into Egypt, no mention is made of the horse; but he is mentioned as being in that country in the time of Joseph, the great-grandson of the patriarch. Abram was the fifth only from Peleg, the founder of the family, brother to Joktan; and Hamyar, from whom, doubtless, the best race of horses in Africa takes its name, was sixth in descent. Supposing Abram and Hamyar to have been contemporaries, there would have been ample time for the horse to have been introduced into Egypt from Arabia, and to have been established, the period being rather over two hundred years. Abram went into Egypt about 1920 B.C.; and the horse is first mentioned in the Bible, 1702 B.C. But there is an indirect mention of the horse. Anah discovered mules in the wilderness, while feeding the asses of Zibeon. This, it must be remembered, was in Arabia, although in the northern or north-eastern part, and the date would either be 1840 B.C. or 1760 B.C. The former would be the more correct date if I be right in the surmise that this Anah was the daughter of Zibeon and mother of Esau's wife, Aholibamah; but in either case it would be a considerable time prior to the first mention of the horse in Egypt.

A stray horse of the Sabæans may have been the cause of the phenomenon, which was evidently accidental, and not, as now, by a perversion of man's; or the accident may have happened as horses were being sent from Arabia into Egypt.

Besides, Scripture clearly indicates that the horse was in Arabia at a very early period by the description of him in the Book of Job, allowed by most to be a work of the highest antiquity, considered by many the oldest extant, believed to have been originally in Arabic, and afterwards translated into Hebrew. When did Job live, where, and of what race was he? One thing is certain: he was a worshipper of the true God, and his acts of worship were according to those of the days of Noah. Job is described as living in the land of Uz. Uz was the name of one of the grandsons of Seir the Horite, who inhabited the land before Esau's days, and probably given to that part of the country to which Uz departed, and not the district known as Mount Seir, somewhere in Arabia, and in the northern part, and was equally accessible to the Chaldeans as to the Sabæans, the southern Arabs; which would indicate that portion of Arabia occupied by Ishmael's children, 'from Havilah unto Shur, that is before Egypt, as thou goest towards Assyria,' reaching from just north of Mount Sinai to the south of Babylonia, and just north of the Persian Gulf. May not Job have been a descendant of Ishmael, and living even in the days of Abraham? The names of Ishmael's sons are given, but not of his grandsons. One of those sons was Tema; one of Job's friends was a

Temanite. He certainly was an inhabitant of Arabia. It is probable he lived as early as the times of Abraham, and, as his possessions were attacked by both Arabs and Chaldeans, that he was living in the land of the Ishmaelites, a considerable portion of which would be desert. The Sabæan descendants of Joktan, in going north from Kahtan, perhaps taking the very same route that the Sabæan Arabs do now annually, fell upon Job's asses and oxen simultaneously as the Chaldeans took off his camels, although the events did not perhaps take place quite in the same place. In the thirty-ninth chapter of the Book of Job the occupation of the horse in Arabia is shown: he is a war-horse and hunter. In the eighteenth verse, in speaking of the ostrich (a bird of Arabia), 'What time she lifteth up herself on high, she scorneth the *horse and his rider,*'—shows he is *ridden*, not driven, as among the Egyptians and other nations; his avocation then was the same as at the present day. The grand description of the horse recounted to Job, so universally admired, and essentially descriptive of the Arabian horse, and so vividly pourtraying him to the mind, does not admit of a doubt that he was then a native of Arabia, and most probably was not altogether unknown to Job.

The Arabs are a people who have existed from the earliest times. Many ancient nations have passed away, new ones risen and also disappeared, but the Arabs still exist, and are the same as four thousand years ago. May we not well believe that the wisdom and power that have kept a people through so many centuries, and preserved them unchanged, which ordained the plan of the Ark and the scheme for replenishing the earth, have ordered and directed the horse into Arabia, to a climate and soil peculiarly adapted to him and to the retention of his primal beauty, vigour, and attributes, under charge of a people who have themselves withstood the changes of the world, to be preserved from all the causes tending to deterioration and degeneracy? Is it not more reasonable to believe that by these means the horse has been preserved very nearly in his original perfection, than that he should have been bred up from a poor miserable animal such as is seen in the highlands of Central Asia, and showing very little of the true character of the horse. 'Facilis descensus Averni' is a very true saying, but it is indeed a difficult thing to ascend and to bring back qualities that have been lost. Besides, we have the most sure warranty that the horse, as all other things, was created perfect; and he, as others, was pronounced to be 'very good.' This truth seems either to be forgotten or overlooked when people talk about improving upon any original species. Do they think man by his skill could breed a better lion or tiger? Has the skill of man during four thousand years succeeded in arriving at so perfect a form or model as the Arabian horse? A most important part has the Arabian horse already played in improving and invigorating the various degenerate breeds of horses scattered over the whole earth, but none have attained unto his perfection; and there may be yet work in store for him.

There are numerous instances mentioned of the horse leaving Arabia for other parts of the world, but no account of his having been imported into that country as an unknown animal, subsequently to the dispersion from Babel. The original inhabitants of Arabia, the sons of Joktan or Kahtan, founded kingdoms and built cities. Yarab, one son, had the province of Yemen, and another son, Jorham, became King of Hejaz. His posterity continued to reign as kings until the time of Ishmael, when either the Ketanic princes were expelled, or the two peoples became one by intermarriage. At this period the kingly rule was changed, in a great measure at all events, for the patriarchal, as among the Bedouin of the present day. Yet in the days of Moses the Ishmaelites were possessed of castles and towns, and towns of considerable extent with castles and palaces are still numerous in Arabia. All Arabs are not Bedouin.[1] Arabia, having been cut off from neighbouring countries where not separated by sea, by a girdle of desert, and by outposts of watchful Bedouin, has preserved its breed of horses as well as its independence, and has never been thoroughly subjugated by any.

It has been stated that celebrated as Persian horses afterwards became, there were very few of them, and those inferior until the time of Cyrus; and he greatly encouraged the breeding of horses. It is very probable

[1] A high state of civilisation was enjoyed by the early Arabians—perhaps that of the antediluvian world; for some of the works of Abd-Shems, the great-grandson of Joktan, still remain, and are perhaps capable of restoration.

that Arabian blood was used by Cyrus for that purpose, and that the Arabian then first became the means of establishing the reputation of the Persian horse, as very many centuries later he made that of the English. In the reign of Neriglissar, King of Babylon, who succeeded Evil-Merodach, and preceded Nabonadius or Belshazzar, there was war between the Babylonians and Persians; Neriglissar was at the head of 20,000 cavalry, with infantry in proportion, and had numerous contingents from other powers. Among these it is mentioned in history that Marogdas the Arabian conducted 10,000 horse. Neriglissar and his allies were totally defeated by Cyrus. It is probable the conqueror was struck with the horses of the Arab contingent, and some, besides, may have fallen into his hands. Arabia may have supplied Babylon also with horses, although doubtless degeneracy had taken place, owing to the use of chariots; and about eighteen years later, when Cyrus besieged and took Babylon, he would have the opportunity of passing them over into Persia, besides, perhaps, of opening some communication with the Arabs.

What was the occupation or calling of Jonadab, the son of Rechab (the son of the rider), who was not of the children of Israel, and how came he to be the friend of Jehu? It is possible and quite consistent to presume he was the medium in those days of horses being passed from Arabia into Palestine, as they are at the present day into India. In other words, it is very likely Jonadab was the merchant of the day who provided Arab horses for Joram's Court and the officers of his army. And who more likely than such an one to be the friend and welcomed companion of the fierce and impetuous Jehu, who *rode* after Ahab, and was well known for his furious driving? The father of Rechab may have performed like services for King Solomon. The Rechabites were Midianites, descended from Abraham and Keturah, and some imagine from that family of Midianites whose forefather was Hohab, brother-in-law to Moses, and dwelt among the Israelites; but in the time of Jeremiah, as the house of the Rechabites went up to Jerusalem only from fear of the army of the Chaldeans, and as they were forbidden to live in houses, to plant, or sow, they evidently were to some extent nomads. Be that as it may, they were Midianites, and these were very early associated and fused with the Ishmaelites, also descended from Abraham, who were intermingled with the ancient Arabians of Ketanic race. That the Midianites were mingled with the Ishmaelites is gathered from the facts mentioned in Genesis. The merchants trading with Egypt in the days of Jacob, and to whom his brethren sold Joseph for twenty pieces of silver, are sometimes described as Midianites, and at others Ishmaelites; although in those days associated, and to some extent one people, it is possible the Ishmaelites were more addicted to wandering and predatory habits, and the Midianites to trading. The former being the first to be associated with the Arabs might have opportunities of acquiring Arab horses; and their kinsmen, the Midianites, being traders, passed them off into

Egypt; which is not at all an improbable means of the horse being taken into Egypt. If the Ishmaelites, in any of the predatory raids, captured horses, they might be glad of such a ready market for them as Egypt. I don't want to insist upon this view, but the Midianite merchants evidently were in the habit of trading with Egypt before the horse is first mentioned. Whether the horse was taken from Arabia into Egypt or originally taken there by Mizraim, it is a country in which the horse would degenerate, and become of larger and heavier build; thus more adapted for harness and chariot work, and another reason why King Solomon should obtain horses from Egypt besides the easy access and his peculiar affinity for that country. The Hebrews had two different words for the horse, one to denote the chariot, the other the riding horse; the former horse was much heavier and larger.

APPENDIX TO THE FIRST CHAPTER.

The causes of degeneracy among horses in other countries than Arabia—The external changes which would ensue—The Arabian still a distinct breed—Additional reason why Arabia was the habitat of the horse.

WHETHER it be supposed or admitted that there were other breeds, or, rather, that the horse was domesticated by several families of mankind about the same time, or whether the horse immediately found his way into Arabia after the Flood, and from thence the race was distributed over the earth, it may be well to show causes that may have produced degeneracy.

The following appear to be some of the most probable:—

Making the horse an animal for draught, using him as a beast of burthen; neglect and the effect of neglect, more especially in cold, damp, and uncongenial climates; and by intermixture of alien species such as the ass and quagga.

Of all nations, the Arabs alone seem to have kept the horse for the purpose for which he was doubtless intended—for riding, not as a beast of draught; other ancient nations used him for harness as well as for saddle. The use of chariots was very general. If we now consider a horse used for draught as spoiled for the saddle, what would be the consequence in a few generations if he were exclusively used for harness work? Would there not be naturally a gradual alteration of structure? Would not his action become materially changed? Undoubtedly great modification would take place; he would become heavier and more upright in the shoulders, would lose his natural easy and graceful carriage, his active and light step, his springiness and elasticity. Again, taken into districts and countries uncongenial to him, uncared for and neglected, a change would very soon take place. If in low, damp, but fat lands, where there was no lack of food, he would soon assume a large, heavy, and bulky frame; but with a loss of vigour, courage, fibre, muscle, density of bone, and compactness of frame, assuming more the characteristic of the fatted ox. If uncared for and starved in damp and cold climates, he would assume a small, wasted, and ill-shaped form. In a cold, but dry climate—such as the highlands of Central Asia and steppes of Russia—allowed to run wild and uncared for, he would become small and often ill-formed, but would retain much of his original spirit and endurance, with density of bone, and much wire and soundness of constitution.

But chief among the causes of decay would be the intermixture of species, as in breeding mules: '*Thou shalt not let thy cattle gender with a diverse kind*' (Leviticus, 19th chapter, 19th verse). For a mare which has once produced a mule cannot again produce a horse—the offspring would invariably partake more or less of the strange breeds. An instance is cited in 'Blaine's Rural Sports.' A thorough-bred mare that had bred to a quagga, subsequently breeding to a horse, the offspring took after the quagga. Experience has taught me that if a mare which has produced a mule has produce afterwards by a horse, the stock always possesses asinine properties, in form, by elongated ears, a heavy head, stripes about the legs and body, contracted feet, and is more or less asinine in temper and character. What else but destruction to the race would be the result if mares who had bred mules, and their after-progeny by horses, were allowed to breed to horses? The striped animals we even now sometimes see are thus easily accounted for.

But the Arabian horse is still a distinct breed, without any sign of degeneracy or of admixture; he is certainly one by himself, nor have any been able to breed up to such a state of perfection or to attain to so perfect a model. I defy any one to point out any feature in the Arabian horse that may have been derived from other breeds, whereas you can trace Arabian blood almost in every breed of horses, and detect his features in a greater or less degree in every kind of horse of breeding, and more or less as it is good and valuable. This appears to me to be a striking instance of the pure and unmixed character of the Arabian horse; and, if pure and unmixed, of the antiquity of his race. Surely it is more reasonable to believe that the horse went southwards from Ararat to a congenial climate, than that he should go north-easterly to Central Asia, and was there first domesticated, as supposed by Colonel Hamilton Smith —to an uncongenial climate; on the other hand, if the horse first multiplied, and his offspring became dispersed and was domesticated in Bactria, the higher valleys of the Oxus, in Cashmere, or in Central Asia, and perhaps simultaneously in several regions, why exclude Arabia? Again, if the horse were not taken into Egypt by Mizraim, or domesticated there simultaneously with other countries, it is more easy to believe he should have been taken from Arabia into Egypt than that herds or troops of wild horses should find their way across so vast an extent of country as from Central Asia to Egypt, many parts of which would be inhabited, for we have no indication or record of any exodus from Central Asia to Egypt between the dispersion at Babel and 1702 B.C. to account for the horse having been taken thence by Man. Moreover, during so long a period (there were 589 years between the Deluge and when the horse is first mentioned in Egypt, according to the chronology in our authorised version of the Scriptures, which gives the lowest calculation), the horse coming from the wilds of Central Asia would have, in all probability, undergone considerable changes, but in Job's time the horse in Arabia was in his grandest form.

Noah found grace in the sight of God, and was saved with his house to perpetuate the race of man. He was not only a just man, but was found 'perfect in his generations' (Genesis, chap. vi. verse 9). This I read simply as it is put, not as it is very generally supposed to mean, that Noah was a godly and an upright man. It is written before that he was a *just* man. I think it implies that Noah and all his ancestry had kept themselves perfect, had not formed alliances with 'the daughters of men,' nor taken 'them wives of all which they chose,' but his generations were to be found entirely in Seth. The whole of Noah's house was saved, which consisted of eight souls, for it is not recorded that he had sons and daughters besides Shem, Ham, and Japhet, which is mentioned in the case of former patriarchs. The race of man was to be carried on after the Deluge by a family which had no ancestral imperfections beyond that inherited from Adam. Surely it may be believed that the animals which the Almighty *caused* to come unto Noah, 'to keep them alive' for the purpose of replenishing the earth, were also perfect in their generations, and for like reasons.

The horse being created good, the most perfect specimens being preserved at the general destruction by the Deluge, it is not inconsistent to suppose the same care might further provide that some portion of the race should be kept perfect and from the things tending to degeneracy. Now, four thousand years after the Flood, we find the horse in Central Asia in a degenerate form ; in Arabia in primeval beauty.

CHAPTER II.

Description of the Arabian horse—Objection taken to the description—Argument in support of the description—More minute description of the Arabian horse—Described by different people—Some exceptions against the Arabian—The horse defended—Proofs offered in defence.

'Hast thou given the horse strength? hast thou clothed his neck with thunder?

Canst thou make him afraid as a grasshopper? the glory of his nostrils *is* terrible.

He paweth in the valley, and rejoiceth in *his* strength: he goeth on to meet the armed men.

He mocketh at fear, and is not affrighted; neither turneth he back from the sword.

The quiver rattleth against him, the glittering spear and the shield.

He swalloweth the ground with fierceness and rage: neither believeth he that *it is* the sound of the trumpet.

He saith among the trumpets, Ha, ha; and he smelleth the battle afar off, the thunder of the captains, and the shouting.'—*Job*, chap. xxxix.

NOTWITHSTANDING the appearance of the Arabian is generally supposed to be well known, this history would not be complete unless his features and characteristics were set forth. And there may still be some who do not know him, and therefore may be unable to recognise him in the above sublime description.

It must be remembered it is not Job who speaks, nor are the words those of man; Job is standing dumb before his Maker, and the words are those of the Almighty, spoken from out of the whirlwind. I find objection has been taken to the passage in the description of the horse of Arabia, 'Hast thou clothed his neck with thunder?' and that it should be his beautiful mane, as no meaning can be attached to clothing the neck with thunder. I beg to differ entirely from this; great force is given, and, I think, the exact idea intended to be conveyed is expressed by the word thunder, which 'the beautiful mane' would not at all express, and which would quite alter the grandeur of the whole description.

Thunder conveys the idea of great force, awe, and majesty; it is lightning, and is emitted with terror. What term could more aptly express the force, strength, and beauty of the Arabian horse's neck, especially when under excitement, and the whole description is of him in an excited state? A neck of a perfect arch, with immense swelling muscles, a splendid large throat, and windpipe of extraordinary capacity, and all set off by his beautiful flowing but light and fine mane, darting out, as the writer has sometimes seen it, like flashes of electricity, and covering the horse, as it were, with a glory; his eyes glowing and emitting flashes of fire and light; his nostrils curled up and almost turned inside out; the whole head seemingly expressed by eyes and nostrils, and that set on, or, as it were, darting forth from his neck of thunder. The description conveys to my mind and senses a true and vivid picture of that which my own eyes have seen.

The Arabian is a horse of the highest courage, in stature about 14 hands 2 inches,[1] a horse of length,

[1] More often a little under than over.

power, and substance, combined with the elastic and the sinuous-like movement of the serpent. He is a very perfect animal; he is not exaggerated—in some parts large; meagre and diminished in others. There is a balance and harmony throughout his frame not seen in any other horse; the quintessence of all good qualities in a compact form.

The beauty of head, ears, eyes, jaw, mouth, and nostrils, should be seen to be appreciated; the ears small, but sufficiently open, pricked, and altogether well-formed; the head short from the eye to the muzzle, broad and well-developed above; the eye peculiarly soft and intelligent when quiescent, emitting light and fire when roused or excited, but very different to the strained wild look, and pained, staring expression often seen in European horses; the nostril long and well chiselled, and crisp in appearance and to the touch, and capable of great distension; the neck is a model of strength and grandeur, of which he can make a perfect arch. One feature, the throat, is particularly large and well developed; it is loose and pliant when at rest, and much detached from the rest of the neck. This feature is not often noticed—indicative not only of good wind, but of the capability of prolonged exertion without distress; great width between the jaws; shoulders of a slope rarely seen in English horses, but more powerful, longer, deeper, and stronger at the base by the withers; lighter at the points. He is deep in the chest, the appearance of which is diminished by his big and deep ribs; back short, loins of immense power, and quarters long and strong, the whole beautifully turned; tail set on high and grandly carried in an arch, powerful in the gaskins; hocks and knees very good and large; these points much larger than seen in the European horse, not only in proportion to height, but often really so. Arms long, legs short, hard, and clean; large tendons and ligaments; pasterns sufficiently long, large, powerful, and springy; fetlock joints well developed, affording room for the advantageous attachment of ligaments; feet tough, sound, and good, and rather deep. An honest heart, a skin as soft as silk, and a coat like satin.

There is no weediness in the Arab; his splendid barrel will at once convince a judge of his wonderful constitution, and gives the expanse necessary for the play of heart and lungs; great power and ability to carry weight. Stand in front of him; you will see the swell and barrel of chest expanding far beyond his shoulders and width of breast. Look at him from behind; his great back ribs extend far beyond his haunches on either side, whereas in the generality of English horses their flat sides are contained within the width of the breast, and are hidden from view when you stand directly in front; and so, when you stand behind, are the back ribs hidden by the quarters. This was not formerly the case. In examining a sketch of Eclipse, drawn from measurements taken by M. St. Bel, the swell of the barrel is seen to extend beyond the breast and shoulders, showing at once how correct is the opinion that the modern horse has deteriorated in outward form.

There is nothing more beautiful to contemplate than

the Arabian horse; not only does he exhibit perfect symmetry, but he is a fit emblem of nobility, generosity, and courage.

The formation of the Arabian is so perfect, there is nothing to spare, no waste; his form is one essentially of utility: the space for the seat of the rider is sufficient, and at once fixes his true position; the weight is therefore carried on that part most adapted for it. The rest of his frame is taken up with the powers of progression. Nature, the unerring artist, has not made a mistake, and man with his improvements has not had the opportunity of spoiling him. If he be carefully examined, it will be found that all the limbs of progression are longer and better placed than in any other horse; the scapulæ, haunches, thighs, and arms are all longer, which, added to the power of great flexion, give great extension, and will explain how the stride of the Arabian, although under 15 hands, is, at all events, greater in proportion to his size than that of any other horse.

Whether we look at the Arabian as a whole, or analyse his points one by one, you can arrive at no other conclusion than that he is an animal of perfect form. It has been truly remarked, the longer he is looked at, and the more minutely he is examined, the more enraptured one becomes, and convinced one is looking at something genuine. Can this be said of any other horse?

It has been said our thorough-bred horse resembles most the Arabian in the form of his figure, his limbs, his head, and his countenance. It would be strange if he did not to a very considerable extent, considering the important part the Arabian has had in his origin, but our horse *certainly* bears the marks of a mixed race. Let us look at some of the points in which a difference may be seen between the Arabian and his descendant, the English horse, where a departure from the pure model has taken place. In the Arabian, the head, countenance, ears, eyes, mouth, jaws, are inimitable, and are not at all approached in beauty by any other breed ; his neck is more beautiful and grander, and far more powerful. The shoulders of the Arabian are stronger than those of the English horse ; the scapulæ are broader at the base, and have a greater inclination backwards ; are of a better shape. Englishmen think the Arabian's a heavier shoulder ; it is really, although a more powerful, a lighter shoulder than that of the English horse. English horses are very thin, narrow, and undeveloped about the withers ; the latter are often high to a fault, but the bases of the scapulæ almost meet ; whereas the Arabian horse shows some thickness there, and can better support weight ; but the English horse is heavier at the shoulder points, and is much wider across the breast than the Arabian—a formation similar to the bull-dog ; it is a weak and heavy shoulder compared with the Arabian's. This broad and heavy breast is a fault I have frequently seen animadverted upon by a warm supporter of our English horse. The Arabian will be seen to barrel and swell out immediately behind the arms—the English horse is flat there. Here is a direct departure from the advantageous form of the original pure blood.

There has also been considerable alteration in the direction and form of the haunch, which, besides being a loss of power, is also a sign of want of breeding. The loins and quarters of the Arabian are more beautiful and far more powerful; they can hardly be called his greatest characteristics, but yet an Arabian might be known by his hind quarters. Another point, the pasterns, which in the Arabian are oblique and yielding, are strong and large in comparison with those of an English thorough-bred horse, as are all other joints. Youatt says: 'In the formation of the shoulder, next to that of the head, the Arab is superior to any other breed.' Again: 'The shoulder-blade has *its proper* inclination backwards. It is thickly clothed with muscle, but without the slightest appearance of heaviness.' The same author says: 'The chest of the Arab *may, perhaps,* be considered too narrow, that being the opinion of the uninitiated, or of those who have studied an imperfect and inferior model, whose judgment has been thereby perverted. *But,*' says the same writer, 'behind the arms the barrel generally swells out, and leaves sufficient room for the play of the lungs.' Youatt is still more emphatic when stating the advantages of this formation, which gives a broad deep *chest*: 'It is to the mixture of Arabian blood that we principally owe this *peculiar* and *advantageous* formation of the chest of the horse. The Arab is light, *some* would say too much so before, but immediately behind the arms the barrel almost invariably swells out, and leaves plenty of room *where it is most wanted for the play of the lungs*, and at the same time where the weight does not press so exclusively on the fore legs, and expose the feet to concussion and injury.' This confirms what has been stated of the perfect symmetry in the Arabian; everything is in its proper place.

To fully appreciate the perfection of the Arabian horse, to the knowledge of a horseman that of an anatomist and painter should be added. By making studies of him with the pencil it is found with surprise how large a horse he is, and the difficulty there is of keeping him within the canvas or paper, and you become assured of the trueness of his proportions.

Mr. Gifford Palgrave thus describes the Arab horses in the Imaun's stables at Riad: 'Their stature was indeed somewhat low. I do not think that any came fully up to fifteen hands—fourteen appeared to me about their average; but they were so exquisitely well shaped, that want of greater size seemed hardly, if at all, a defect. Remarkably full in the haunches, with a shoulder of a slope so elegant as to make one, in the words of an Arab poet, "go raving mad about it." A little, a very little, saddle-backed, just the curve which indicates springiness without any weakness; a head broad above, and tapering down to a nose fine enough to verify the phrase of "drinking from a pint pot," did pint pots exist in Nejed; a most intelligent and yet a singularly gentle look; full eye; sharp, thorn-like little ear; legs, fore and hind, that seemed as if made of hammered iron, so clean, and yet so well twisted with sinew; a neat round hoof, just the requisite for hard ground; the tail set-on, or rather thrown out, at a perfect arch; coat smooth, shining, and light; the mane long, but not overgrown nor heavy. Their appearance justified all reputation, all value, all poetry.

'But if asked what are, after all, the specially distinctive points of the Nejdee horse, I should reply, the slope of the shoulder, the extreme cleanness of the shank, and the full rounded haunch; though every other part, too, has a perfection and a harmony unwitnessed (at least by my eyes) anywhere else.

'The peculiar obliquity of the shoulder-blade gave them an easy, springy movement, which, combined with their splendid barrel, immense haunches, superbly set tail, delicate muzzle, and magnificent crest, made them the beau ideal of a horse.'

The following is the description of Major Gwatkin's Arab horse, Barefoot, considered by Mr. Elliott as the best specimen of the Arabian he had met with in India. It is very characteristic, and is almost identical with the preceding more general description: 'Barefoot is of the Nejdee caste, eight years old, 14 hands 2 inches; is a silvery grey, with a dark skin, blood head, full eye, large throttle, light neck; the shoulders are flat, with the muscular lines very distinct; withers well raised; a good arm, leg flat, and the sinews large and well detached from the bone; pastern of a moderate length. His back and loins are particularly beautiful, and convey the idea of great strength. His quarters are finely turned and very muscular. His temper is exceedingly good. When led out to start, he appears to great advantage, full of fire, yet very temperate; and when at work no horse could evince more vigour and determined courage. Other similar examples might be shown of the Arabian as known in India, and among them the beautiful and equally good Little Honeysuckle.'

A gentleman to whom I am much indebted, and who has for many years been in constant intercourse with the Bedouin Sheiks from Nejed, thus speaks of the Arabian: 'The Arab, although less swift for a short distance, is certainly stouter than the English thorough-bred horse; his stride is greater in proportion to their size.'

The English thorough-breds are certainly flatter, more lathy, and of less swelling development than the best Arabians. The Arabians have longer shoulder-blades in proportion to height, and it is only the first blood of England that comes near the Arabian in obliquity. Muscle starts out of the Arabian in a way I never saw in the best trained English racer. Bone is of a closer texture, more heavy when a cubic inch of each is weighed. First-class Arabians have as large hocks as English horses; their feet as a rule larger. All good Arabians have the same high, full, and long quarters, and tail set-on high and carried well. Nejed is a country where the best horses are to be found.

Abd-el-Kader thus describes the Arabian: 'Every horse of noble race fascinates the eyes and rivets the gaze of the enthusiastic spectator. In a pure bred Arabian the moral and physical qualities are inseparable one from the other.' The truth and faithfulness of this cannot fail to be recognised by any who know the Arabian horse.

I give an account of an Arabian sent as a present to the late Emperor of the French from Abd-el-Kader, after his residence had been fixed at Damascus: it was written, no doubt, by one more conversant with European horses than Arabians. 'The horse Emir is eight years old, colour brown, with a very silky skin, three white fetlocks; some white, but not too much, about his face. He has some white spots about the size of a small pea on his neck and shoulders. He stands fourteen hands one inch high, has a good, long, lean head, well set-on; ears slender, his eye mild and intelligent, his mane and tail light and the hair fine; a handsome straight, strong neck longer than one generally sees with other Arabs; his shoulders are long and well laid-in, each of those points showing much quality. He has great legs and quarters, ribs and back wide to a degree; hoofs black, strong, wide at the heels, and deep; joints large; knees and hocks very good. He is all over a remarkably strong, thick-made horse; but to my taste too thick to be speedy, and sinks a little too much upon his fetlocks, but we cannot have perfection; his action is more elastic than might be expected from a horse of his build and strength. He is as gentle as a sheep, without being dull; he looks like what we would call a craving but very aristocratic animal.'[1]

[1] This horse has been described as of the race Kohel-Obaion; probably his sire was Keheilan and his dam Abeyan, or *vice versâ*. See account of various families, Chap. III., Part 3.

I venture to offer a few remarks. The writer is at a loss to understand how so strong and powerful a horse can have speed, although he sees and admits his action to be elastic. If he had been more conversant with Arabians, he would have known that the rare combination of points to be found only in the Arabian, permits of a horse being strong, powerful, enabled to carry weight, and with good speed, and all done with light and elastic action. And why object to his springy and elastic pasterns,—the means provided by nature to secure his good action, and preserve him from accidents? Has not rather the European eye been perverted by studying a false and imperfect model? I think, too, he must have been mistaken in the *long* head. The Flying Dutchman, who was more distinguished for elastic action and for springy pasterns than perhaps any other English race horse, was a sound horse; and I have seen it noticed that upon one occasion, when trainers were only allowing their horses to take gentle canters, and for short distances, Fobert was sending the Dutchman over the *hard* ground four-mile gallops; but, as was remarked, *he* was one *of the very few sound ones.*

But the Arab is so small! is the remark made by many of his detractors. He is low in stature, but is no weed. He is not a small, but really a large horse. Those who do not know the Arab cannot understand this; they say, if a horse 14½ hands has as much power as one 15½ or 16 hands, he must be out of proportion; they are ever guided by the English standard. They see the pretty galloways or ponies in London or Paris about

14 hands or a little over, perhaps capable of carrying eight or nine stone; and therefore argue, the Arab being about the same height, it is the same with him; but Arabs are master of more than a light weight, and have done some wonderful things under very heavy weights. A member of the Royal College of Veterinary Surgeons thus speaks of an Arab 14 hands 1 inch, he had the opportunity of seeing a few years ago; he might not have seen many Arabs, yet his knowledge of anatomy enabled him at once to appreciate the horse: 'I consider him better able to carry fourteen stone than many horses that measure fifteen hands, and more elastic and easy to ride; his hind quarters are longer and bigger than some horses at sixteen hands. I believe him to be *the most perfect horse I have ever seen.*' Here we have the acknowledgment from a professional man—who, after some thirty years' experience, during which period he must have seen some of the *élite* of England—that the one little Arab stranger, not a selected horse, was the most perfect specimen of the equine race he had met with; and further, a declaration that in an animal of 14 hands 1 inch actual greater size was found than in many of 16 hands, yet with a *perfect* form. A small horse is not necessarily a weed; and one apparently very large may be in reality a small horse, may be light and weedy; another may be big, coarse, and weedy. An overgrown horse, although he may have powerful shoulders and quarters, big limbs and large bone, if he fails in his middle piece and loins—which is very often the case—is weedy. He is not in harmony; he lacks

the constitutional powers to work his large frame. A small light horse, with light and sloping shoulders, with powerful quarters and thighs, and even with great depth of chest, may also be a weed, from being deficient in barrel, flat and narrow instead of a swelling development, and faulty in the loins. These horses may have speed, they may be prepared and win a race, but they are not the horses that would have won races a hundred years ago.

It may be called heresy, but it is nevertheless true, that very many of our celebrated modern racers are and have been nothing more nor less than weeds.

Others have said, the Arab's weak points are his shoulders, and his paces are bad; nothing less than execrable. The paces of a horse (except the gallop) are very much what the rider makes them.

Arabs have little or no trouble taken with their education. In India they are taught to walk badly, to step at a short contracted pace, by their being constantly, and sometimes for weeks together, led by their syces (grooms) at the rate of about two miles an hour. It is hardly fair to blame a horse for the very faults man has taught him. I suppose one would not be far wrong in saying that ninety out of every hundred men who ride are carried as their horses choose to go—not as their riders like. If a horse trots, his rider is content to go at a trot; if he canters, the rider concludes he cannot trot. So it is with the Arab; he has been taught a cramped action before at a walk. When his owner gets up, instead of correcting the errors that have been forced upon his horse, he contents himself by saying no Arab can walk. The horse has probably never been tried at a trot; therefore it is said he cannot trot. I affirm that the Arabian can walk, trot, and gallop. I have possessed some that would walk five miles an hour, and certainly one that could do that pace at the rate of six or more miles in the hour. The fastest trotter I ever rode, or perhaps have ever seen, unless among trained trotters, was an Arab.

Even the detractors of the Arab allow that he will gallop at speed with ease and in safety over broken and rough ground. This is certain proof that his shoulders are not faulty, and a most incontestable proof that they are very perfect. Besides this, I will give two illustrations which will, I think, convince any *horseman* that the Arab *must* have good and perfect shoulders. Most must have noticed when riding on the grass by the side of roads, how constantly their horses are putting their feet into the grips, or on the edge of them, which have been cut to carry off the water, and which, it would appear, they were incapable of avoiding, jerking and shaking their own limbs, and making it unpleasant for their riders. I have known Arabs, on the contrary, either at a canter or a trot, avoid these grips and obstacles by a most nimble management of their legs either extending one shoulder and leg beyond the grip or putting one foot neatly down before concluding the usual length of pace. The other is the ability Arabs have of playing with their forefeet, even when at a tolerably smart gallop. If a bird or insect, no matter how small, suddenly flies across their path, without stopping they will make a pat at it, like a kitten playing with a ball. Such feats, I hold, cannot possibly be performed except by a horse with good shoulders and a free use of them; bad shoulders and galloping bring the legs to grief. See the amount of galloping the Arab's legs can stand.

Galloping one of my own Arabs at more than three-quarter speed on the race-course at Amballah, the horse put his near fore foot into a fox's or rat's hole—such holes were very numerous; this let him down in depth to his knee, but did not bring him down—it scarcely made a difference in his stride—good shoulders or bad.

I will give another instance, which, I think, displays not only the high courage of the Arabian, but his wonderful power and activity. The Arab I was riding, jackal-hunting, would have been considered an old horse in England. He could not have seen less than twenty summers, had been a racer, had gone through two campaigns as a charger, but his legs were as straight and clean as a foal's. After a kill, when riding slowly homewards, we came to the bank of a nullah. Some thought the bottom looked suspicious. I pushed my horse down, and was immediately up to the hips of my horse in quicksands. I would have got off if I could, but the horse never gave me a chance; his bounds and springs can only be described as astonishing; he lifted himself straight up out of the treacherous soil over and over again, only to be again engulfed; still he did not give up, nor fall over, or succumb, and finally landed on a sounder bit. We escaped. I could not have believed any animal could have displayed such strength; formerly on several occasions I had been bogged on Dartmoor, and have subsequently on forest lands in England, but I never found a horse behave under me like the old Arab. Five minutes afterwards there was a whimper, an indication of a find; the gallant old horse's head was up, his beautiful little ears pricked; he was dancing on his legs, anticipating another gallop.

As to the action of the Arabian, it is very well described by the writer of an able article who signed himself 'Picador.' 'Sit easily and flexibly on him, put your hands down, and set him going, and then you will experience a sensation delightful to the man who really can ride: he will bound along with you with a stride and movement that gives you the idea of riding over india-rubber.'

CHAPTER III.

The boundaries of the Arab people—The Arabian horse and his habitat further discussed—Arab horses in Africa; but horses called Barbs not generally of pure Arabian blood—Confusion existing as to the Arabian horse, owing to the use of improper terms—Egypt and Turkey not the habitat of the Arabian—Different terms explained—One breed of Arabians—The several families discussed, and the tribes who possess them—Apparent discrepancies in the accounts of travellers explained.

'Who can tell where the Arab dwelleth, or who has marked out the boundaries of his people?'—*Warburton.*

FROM Diarbekr in the north, to Hadramaut in the south, from the Euphrates and even the Tigris, to the western coast of Africa, is Arabic spoken, more or less; and every part of this vast district is traversed by the Arabs or their descendants.[1] But our present business is with the Arabian horse and his habitat. Mr. Layard mentions the horses of the Shammar tribe who were frequently about him during his excavations at Nineveh, and speaks with the greatest admiration of some of their mares. Sofuk, then their sheikh, was possessed of a mare of matchless beauty, and Kubleh, her dam, was still more celebrated for her speed and powers of endurance, and was known from the sources of Khabour to the end of the Arabian promontory.

[1] It must not be thought that Arabian horses are common, or to be found throughout this district, or wherever Arabic may be spoken.

The Shammar migrated from Central Arabia about two hundred years ago. Being pushed by subsequent emigrations, they crossed the Euphrates, and are to be found principally between that river and the Tigris, known as Mesopotamia. Here we have the Arab and his horse in the most north-eastern district. Mr. Gifford Palgrave speaks of him in Nejed, which is the central highland of Arabia proper; Abd-el-Kader and General Daumas speak of him in Africa, or the most westerly part of the Arab's possessions. But all horses from the north of Africa are not Arabs. Barbs, properly speaking, are common horses on the coasts or northern parts of Africa, of Arabian origin, but of mixed blood, and very inferior, yet are often, although falsely, called Arabs. There is no reason to doubt that the horses of the Sahara are the pure and unmixed descendants of the importation from the parent country; and when in Africa some years ago the writer saw one or two horses, evidently pure Arabian, and entirely different from common Barbs. So, again, on the borders of Syria, in Irak, Khuzistan, and Kurdistan, are to be found horses of mixed blood, generally called Arabs, often sold and bought as such; and being sometimes of *taller growth*, but always less beautiful and far inferior to the Arabian, are often even preferred by the European; and from the eastern side of the Persian Gulf, horses of mixed blood are often passed as Arabs. Could a stranger form a correct idea of the English thorough-bred horse, if he had only seen the hacks let out for hire at our sea-side places of resort?

Much confusion exists with regard to Arab horses. This has arisen partly from the vast districts occupied and traversed by the Arabs, partly from the misapplication of terms and words. A man possessing an Arab horse says he is of such and such a breed, instead of saying, of such a family of the Arabian breed; and therefore it has got about that there are upwards of a hundred different breeds of Arabian horses. It is not unfrequent to hear people speak of horses as Egyptian, Syrian, or Turkish Arabs. If it were intended to convey the idea that such horses were of pure Arab blood, only foaled or bought in those countries, they might be simply styled Arabs; but as it really infers that they are not of pure Arabian blood they should simply be called Egyptian, &c. With the exception of horses sent as gifts very occasionally to the Sultan at Constantinople, or the Viceroy in Egypt, let it be most distinctly understood there are no Arabians in Egypt or Turkey. The Arabian is not the horse of either country. The Egyptian is the degenerated horse of Egypt crossed with the horse of Dongola, the English horse, and also the Arab, and is as mixed as most European breeds.

The terms Nejed or Nejdee, and Anezah, as applied to Arabian horses, have led to much confusion and produced many doubts. It has been generally supposed they implied two separate breeds of horses, rival breeds by some, a superior and inferior by others, or that they were the horses of two great rival tribes. Some will tell you the Nejdee is the only pure Arabian, others that the Anezah is the best.

These doubts and conflicting statements have arisen, I do not doubt, from a want of knowledge of the country of Arabia, and correct information of its people and its horses. Nejed is the name of a country or district in Arabia ; but is neither the name of a breed of horses, nor of any particular tribe ; and probably that district discussed at the commencement of the first chapter, in which the horse was kept free from the causes of degeneracy which has befallen the horse in other parts of the world ; or, as Mr. Palgrave has aptly put it, 'In Nejed is the true birthplace of the Arab steed—the primal type, the authentic model.'

Every horse bred in Nejed, or bred by any of the tribes of Nejed, may be called correctly a Nejdee, or a horse of Nejed ; not, I think, implying any difference in race and blood from an Anezah horse, but solely as a distinction from the horses of other tribes than those of Nejed, such as the Shammar, although they possess horses of the same blood as those in Nejed ; and most distinctly in opposition to all horses of mixed blood on the borders or outskirts of Arabia.

The horses of the Great Anezah and other Bedouin tribes of Nejed, of which there are several (Mr. Palgrave enumerates twelve), are essentially Nejdee horses. The Great Anezah is sub-divided into many families ; and from among them the Gomassa have, perhaps, the best horses in the known world. In describing a horse as an Anezah, or, still further, as a Gomassa, it is not implied that he is not Nejdean, but he is particularised as a Nejdean horse of the Great Anezah tribe, of the

S'bah division of the Gomassa family; in the same way as the English horse, Saunterer, for instance, in male descent, might be described of the Darley Arabian line, of the Waxy family, of the Birdcatcher branch. I am assured that many horses in the stables of the Imaun of the Wahabees have been obtained from the Bedouin, especially the Anezah, either purchased, or by tribute, or as gifts.[1] The blood in Nejed and among other Bedouin is the same.

I believe there is really but one breed of Arabian horses, although many families. There are five principal families, *not breeds*, derived from five celebrated mares. They are usually styled Seglawi, Keheilan, Abeyan, Hadban, and Hamdami. No allusion is intended to the tale of five mares ridden by Mohammed and his followers; which I believe to be a European invention. The Arabian horse existed thousands of years before Mohammed's time; besides, the Arabs say, as was before mentioned, that his one follower rode on a camel.

The Bedouin would scorn any horse or mare that could not be traced back to these five families. Certain specific adjuncts to these names indicate first-class animals, or the best specimens of the five families or varieties; other specific names denote second-class animals; and an absence of a distinguishing name to the generic, implies the animals are of the third class. The numerous divisions that have sprung from these

[1] As the Ibn Sawood, the ruling family of the Wahabees at Riad, is of Anezah origin, the first being a Sheik of the Sebaa, this may be the more readily received.

five families have derived their names from their owners, from the events that made them famous, or from some personal quality: as Seglawi Jedran, from the name of the owner; Keheilan-Abu-Argub (Father of Hocks), Abu-Jenub (Father of Flanks), and Keheilan-ras-el-Fedawi (The Headstrong). This was the family from whence came the renowned Darley Arabian. There is no crossing implied by breeding indiscriminately among the five families, the blood is identical, and the foal takes the name of the variety of the dam; thus a colt or filly whose dam was a Seglawi, and whose sire was Keheilan, would be Seglawi. Animals of the first class are those only which are the produce of both horses and mares of the first class, nor will this alone suffice; for if the colt or filly were possessed of any unlucky marks, or should they fail to come up to a certain standard, they are not considered first-class, are not allowed the specific adjunct of their dam, but drop into the third class, and retain their generic name only. None but first-class horses are allowed for first-class mares, and when an inferior horse (not one of less pure blood) has through inadvertence or by accident covered a mare of the first class, such a mare is herself lost to her class, and becomes of the second, as does her offspring. This is how a second class has been established.

The most esteemed from the five families are Seglawi-Jedran, Keheilan-Adjuz, Abeyan-Sherrak, Hadban-Enzehi, and Hamdami-Simri. The varieties of the Keheilan are the most numerous, and many of them are first-class besides Keheilan-Adjuz, as, for instance, Maneghi-Hedrudj, Keheilan-Abu-Argub, Keheilan-Abu-Jenub, and Keheilan-ras-el-Fedawi.

The second-class Seglawi are Seglawi-Obeiran and Seglawi-Arjibi, formed, as before-mentioned, by accident. So there is one breed of Arabian horses, five distinguished families; most of these divided into three classes. Many of the third class have their own specific adjuncts, and I have no doubt they would amount to over one hundred, but these are not separate *breeds*; and although the blood is the same, one would naturally prefer animals of the select Arab class.

Arabian horses are to be found among most, if not all, of the Bedouin tribes, in greater or less numbers, and also among the resident population in Nejed, but would hardly be so numerous among the latter, as the nobles or wealthy only would possess them. The Imaun of the Wahabees, his sons and officers, have their separate studs.

The five different families of horses are also possessed indiscriminately by different Bedouin tribes, but all do not necessarily possess horses of each variety. The Shammar are principally located in Mesopotamia. The Mawali, a small tribe, are generally to be found between Aleppo, Palmyra, and Damascus; the Weldi on the borders of Mesopotamia; the Weldi Ali always east of Damascus; the Beni-Sachar and Salhaan east of Jerusalem, and on the banks of the Jordan; some few smaller tribes have settled and taken to agriculture.

The Great Anezah, or Anezah proper, describe an

annual circuit. Coming up from Nejed to near Aleppo in the spring they cross the desert to the Euphrates, and return into Nejed for the winter. They are the largest and most powerful of all tribes, and have by far the greatest number of horses. They are divided into several tribes, and these again into sections or subdivisions. The Fedan-Anezah has nine divisions: Mehed, the people of Jedaan (a well-known chief), Tooenis, Ajajara, Roas, Shmeilat, Griebat, Roaba, and Hrisa; this last is, I believe, subdivided. Then there are Jelas, Roala, Seloot, Erfuddi, Shumlan, Hayaza, and Ibu-Haddal; the Amarat, Magin, Serdyeh, Tiar, and Hesenneh. Last, but not the least important among the Anezah, is the Sebaa, with its seven divisions—Duam, Abideh, Ishhoieh, Mooeneh, Gomassa, Mooajeh, and Beaieh. If not the most numerous, they have the reputation of being the wealthiest of all tribes, possessing enormous herds and flocks, and they can muster 12,000 horsemen.

The apparent discrepancy between this account and that which has been frequently asserted and generally accepted, is not difficult of explanation. Some writers have mentioned that there are upwards of one hundred breeds of Arabian horses, but it is generally supposed there are three distinct breeds; the first pure, the second of mixed blood, and the third with no claim to gentle breeding, although, rather contradictorily, it is admitted a good deal of the choice blood is distributed among animals of that breed; and, lastly, that the Nejdean horse is the best or of the highest type.

First, the numerous subdivisions which have been derived from the classes formed from the before-mentioned five celebrated families, and most of them with specific names, would account for the broad assertion that there are numerous *breeds.*

Secondly, the three classes, according to the nice discrimination of the Bedouin (although of the same blood), would explain the statement that there are three *distinct breeds* ; which statement, made in good faith, has nevertheless misled many, and caused much confusion; but only required a little further investigation to get at the bottom of it. The first, stated as pure, from the fact that, except through inadvertence, mares of the first class are never covered by any but accepted stallions of the first class. The second *breed*, mentioned as being of mixed blood, from the fact that mares of the second class are continually being put to horses of the first ; the mares often being sent long distances.

Thirdly, the rather contradictory description that the horses of the third breed have no claim to gentle breeding, although they have a good deal of choice blood distributed among them, is quite explained by the fact that the third class is made up from horses and mares of the first, which have failed in some requirements, and perhaps sometimes from no authentic notice having been taken of their birth, although of the same identical blood.

And fourthly, that the horses of Nejed are best, and reared in the remoter parts of the desert, from the very evident circumstance that the Anezah possess the greatest number, and the best horses in Arabia, and that they do come from Nejed, and that they are indeed a part of the population of Nejed, and when wandering, as a rule keep within the more remote parts of the desert, avoiding as far as possible all intercourse with the Turks, whom they dislike and despise.

Although representatives of the five families are distributed indiscriminately among the different tribes, it is necessary to know where to go for the best of each kind. Keheilans are to be found in all tribes. The Shammar in Mesopotamia have principally Hellawis, which are a third class of Keheilan. Of course there are some horses of the first class in their possession; and these have not been overdrawn by Mr. Layard, for the celebrated Anezah sheik Jedaan rode a mare constantly, which had been given him by the Shammar sheik, because she was unsurpassed in speed and bottom, so that he might not fall into the hands of the Shammar—the two sheiks having been playmates in their boyhood's days. But the Shammar have a bad name. They have Kurds and Persians in their close proximity, who would always be ready to pass off an animal of mixed breed as an Arab.

The number of first-class animals among small tribes, such as the Mowali, must necessarily be small. Formerly at feud with the Anezah, but latterly often on friendly terms with them, they might have an opportunity of acquiring horses, or of breeding from their first-class horses.

The Fedan Anezah is a great fighting tribe, and use

and consume a great number of horses. They have very fine horses, and some of these must sometimes fall into other hands; their consumption in horseflesh is so great that they often have to buy from other tribes. The Roala and Ibu Haddal Anezah are well-horsed tribes; but of all, the Sebaa Anezah is the tribe for horses, and of their seven subdivisions the Gomassa have the reputation of possessing the finest horses in the world. The Seglawi Jedran is found in its greatest perfection among the Gomassa. The Fedan Anezah possess also two families. The Gomassa have also the best Abeyans and the best Maneghi: this latter a first-class subdivision of the Keheilan.

Although horses of equal beauty and perfection are to be found in all five families, the Seglawi Jedran may be the favourite among Bedouin, and, perhaps, the most famous.

PART 3.

CHAPTER I.

The Arabian considered as a racer—Characteristics of Arab racing—His speed considered—Account of various races contested by Arabs in India—Racing sometimes slower in England—The normal speed of Arabs increased by a better system of training—No effort made to secure the importation of the best Arab horse—The European idea of size detrimental to the importation of good Arabs—Ibraheen-bin-Alee and Honeysuckle—The Arabs King David and Antelope.

HAVING discussed both the English horse of the Stud Book and the Arabian—the former having been clearly shown to be nothing more than a registered half-bred, while the latter is the real aristocrat and the true noble, always bearing in mind the necessity of pure breeding for the attainment of great excellence—we will proceed to consider how advantageous it would be to employ the Arabian: first, to establish a pure breed in this country; secondly, how admirably he is adapted to raise the character of half-bred stock for the purpose of field sports and for the army, even supposing that horses of such pure blood might not become available for both such purposes.

First, as a racer. It is said, and will be said again, the Arab is a small animal, and without speed, therefore incapable of either being a racer or of begetting racing stock. This is a frequent assertion. Let us see if it holds good. Our horse which we call thorough-bred, 'our terribly high-bred racer,' is the Arab's half-bred descendant; the Arab has, in fact, made a breed of racers by the infusion of his blood into a very inferior breed. This part of the subject might be dismissed after the following words. Our racer, such as he is, is a living witness of the Arabian's capability to found and create a breed of racers. He has made a breed of racers in spite of the many inferior strains of blood that he has had to combat with; it is only reasonable to believe that had his blood been used alone, with the same advantages in cultivation and selection that have been bestowed upon his half-bred descendant, his pure-bred descendants would have exhibited greater excellence.

As a racer himself the Arabian possesses every natural gift and qualification—courage, docility, temper, endurance, good and untiring action, great determination, nervous energy, and speed; for a horse that can run two miles under Derby Course weights in 3 min. 48 secs. cannot truly be called a slow horse or devoid of speed. The speed exhibited by Arabians on the race-course may be termed their normal speed, in contradistinction to the artificial speed of the English racer, because he has not been bred generation after generation as a racer or for the sole sake of speed; but *such Arab horses as have come to hand* have shown this rate of speed and also ability to maintain a high rate of speed.

The Arab will run an honest and true horse from end to end; he stands training for years; his temper is so good, a large field can be sent from the post without difficulty the first time. Close finishes, severe struggles, dead heats, and not unfrequently dead heats after dead heats, are the characteristics of Arab racing. Open the pages of the 'Oriental Sporting Magazine,' and almost every start of Arabs is described as being got off in capital order the first time of asking—in the usual way, in fact. Then he is so kind and so generous! In his compact form is also contained every requisite for combined speed and strength—the broad, deep, and swelling *chest* (the most desirable for rapid progression), length in the right place, length of shoulders, length of quarters, length in his arms, immense power to work the parts of motion, and great nervous energy to excite the power; and, owing to his true symmetry, he has nothing superfluous to carry. All these points are more conspicuous and more developed in the Arabian than in any other horse. He has more length in proportion to size, and more power, is a bigger, larger, and far more powerful animal than our thorough-bred, in proportion to size. He does not open his mouth and drop his bit when you ask him to do his best. (It is worthy of consideration whether this trait has not been on the increase the last decade or two.) His heart is all right, and in the right place, which, with his sound constitution and his perfect formation, enables him not only to struggle to the end of his race, but to come out day after day.

The best criterion we have of the speed of the Arabian

is from his performances on the Indian turf. There he has met English racers and his descendants from Australia (thorough-bred as our horse); and although his speed has been inferior as a rule, instances are not wanting in which he has been the victor over English horses of racing blood; and even when beaten, has proved his superiority as a horse; for after having struggled with unflinching gameness to the end against greater speed, the vanquished has been none the worse, and has come out the next day, and day after day, and won; whereas the victor or victress has been unable to put in an appearance. But it is argued only second or third-class racers have found their way to India! Will any man be bold enough to say that the best Arabians have ever appeared on an Indian racecourse either? Even there he is under as many disadvantages as the English horse; and his performances, good as they are, can hardly be considered as fair tests of what the speed and running of some Arabians may be; certainly does not limit what it might be brought to, if they were carefully bred for racers for a generation or two. First of all, in India one is dependent for Arabs upon merchants, who import them often without a guarantee as to their antecedents or ancestry; and although some Arabians do go to India, there are many that are called Arabs which are not Arabs. Besides, many of the best that do get there are never seen on a race-course, or do not appear until well in years and accustomed to other work (and it is well known in England bringing an aged horse out, even if he had previously been a racer, proves a failure), their owners keeping them for their own use as hog-hunters, riding-horses, or chargers. Then only *horses* are imported; and as it has been found that English mares run much better than horses in India, it is just possible that Arabian mares might also run better than horses in that country. This is no doubt owing to climate, especially in Bengal, and perhaps Madras, for the often humid climate of Bengal is as great a change for the Arab as to the English horse, or greater; for in Arabia, although under a burning sun, he has been accustomed to a dry, bracing, exhilarating, and peculiarly pure air, unknown in our island. But from among such Arabs as go to India, when running among themselves, can anyone say that they do not possess the highest merits as race-horses? Possessed of speed only inferior, as a rule, to the carefully-bred racers of England, but combined with stoutness, which enables them to run continuously races of any distance in as good time as is often seen in England.

The race-courses in India are measured to a yard, and I believe at the distance of one foot only from the inner circle, thus giving the shortest possible amount of ground a horse can go over. The following instances of time and distance (taken from the 'Oriental Sporting Magazine'), will prove the claim of the Arabian to be considered a race-horse:—At Calcutta, January 1847, the gray Arab horse, The Baron, aged, ran ½ mile, at 8 st. 7 lb., in 54 secs., which is considered the average rate for a ½ mile, the ¼ mile being continually accomplished in 26 secs. But it is recorded that at Soonepoore in 1844, the gray Arab, Sir Hugh, did the first ½ mile for the Soonepoore Cup in 51 secs.; and at the same place and following year the bay Arab Oranmore beat Sir Hugh, doing the ½ mile in 52 secs. At Calcutta, 1847, the bay Arab horse, The Child of the Islands, 6 years, did ¾ mile, carrying 8 st. 7 lb., in 1 min. 21 secs., beating among others the English horse Ignis Fatuus (by Slane out of Deception), the English mare Morgiana, and the New South Wales mare Greenmantle, carrying 9 st. 7 lbs. each. The three quarters were run in 26 secs., 28 secs., 27 secs. At Calcutta, 1847, the bay Arab horse Minuet, 5 years, ran 1 mile in 1 min. 50 secs., carrying 8 st. 3 lbs.; this being the *last* mile of the race, for the Civilian Cup 2¼ miles: Minuet beating among others the English mare Morgiana, and the New South Wales mare Greenmantle without difficulty—the weights are not given. The gray Arab Brag carrying 9 stone, ran a mile at Allyghur in 1845 in 1 min. 51 secs. The Child, carrying 8 st. 13 lbs., also ran a mile in that time at Calcutta, 1847; the same year he ran the same distance in the same time, beating the English mare Cossack Maid, carrying 8 st. 11 lbs., the Arab carrying 8 st. 10 lbs. At Calcutta, 1847, the bay Arab horse Glaucus, aged, ran 1¼ mile, carrying 9 st. 7 lbs., in 2 min. 22 secs. At Calcutta, in 1847, the bay Arab horse, The Child of the Islands, 5 years old, ran 1½ mile, carrying 7 st. 8 lbs., in 2 min. 48 secs., coming home too in a hand gallop. At Calcutta, 1847, the gray Arab horse Elepoo, aged, ran 1¾ mile, carrying 8 st. 4 lbs., in 3 min. 20 secs., beating Morgiana, 9 st. 2 lbs. At Calcutta, in 1848, the grey Arab horse Honeysuckle, about 14 hands 1 inch, ran 2 miles, carrying 8 st., in 3 min. 48 secs., beating the English mare Morgiana, New South Wales mare Greenmantle, and The Child of the Islands, carrying 9 st. This race was the fastest for the distance hitherto run by an Arab. The next month Honeysuckle, carrying 8 st. 11 lbs., ran also 2 miles in 3 min. 50 secs. (several persons making the time 3 min. 48 secs again), beating Minuet, 8 st. 13 lbs., and Elepoo, 7 st. 13 lbs.

At Calcutta, the bay Arab horse Minuet, in 1848, ran 2¼ miles, carrying 8 st. 7 lbs. in 4 min. 19 secs., winning without difficulty, beating The Child of the Islands, the New South Wales mare Greenmantle, and the English mares Morgiana and Cossack Maid at 8 st. 7 lbs., 9 st. 9 lbs., 9 st. 4 lbs., and 8 st. 5 lbs. respectively. At Calcutta, 1841, the grey Arab horse Glendower ran 2½ miles, carrying 8 st. 8 lbs., in 4 min. 53 secs.

At Calcutta January 3, 1846, the bay Arab horse Selim, aged, ran 3 miles, carrying 9 st. 5 lbs., in 5 min. 54 secs. This was the quickest three miles run by an Arab. These instances, showing that the Arabian can maintain nearly his highest rate of speed from end to end in 3 miles, surely prove him to possess the highest qualities of a racer, and show that his natural speed is by no means contemptible. It is remarked, Selim would have proved a first-rate racer, had he been entered young on the Turf; but he was used as a hog-hunter until aged.

The performances of the Arab Gray-leg will give some idea of the continuous running of Arabians. He was 14 hands 1¾ inch in height; he was never out of training for 7 years, from 1861 to 1868; he ran 80 times and won 51 races at all distances, and under all weights. At Bombay, 1864, he won the Forbes Stakes, 2 miles, beating the English mare Shah Rook and the Australian Van Diemen; he also won a handicap 1½ mile, beating the English mare Mary Glen, 9 st. each.

The gray Arab Hermit is another example of speed, weight, carrying power, and continuance. He won during his career 32 races, besides 2 disputed ones, which he had won with ease. At Calcutta, 1862, won the Trades Plate, 1½ mile, carrying 10 st. 4 lbs., beating five others, in 2 min. 56 secs. Next day a cup, with 9 st. 3 lb. up. Then came his celebrated race with the English mare Voltige and three others, two of which, the Walers Sampson and Ellerton, were horses of note; he was beaten by Voltige, it is true, but the Arab was fresh and well the next day, and came out and won his race in style; whereas the English mare declined a fresh encounter. The race for the Trades Cup is thus described:—'They came by the stand, Voltige leading, Sampson second, and Hermit (the Arab) third; having done the first quarter in 26 secs. Almost immediately after, Hermit ran up to the mare, and remained with her, doing the mile in 1 min. 52 secs. Soon after this the others were out of the race, for the two were keeping up the pace and gradually dropping them, passing the mile and half in 2 min. 49 secs. Sampson was quite told out half a mile from home. As they turned the Calcutta corner

Hermit went up and collared the mare, but under persuasion she drew away again slightly, and finished a couple of lengths in advance of the Arab.' The 2 miles were accomplished in 3 min. 46 secs.

The day following he won the Calcutta Stakes, 2 miles. Hermit, Ellerton, Voltige, and Sampson were entered. Both Voltige and Sampson were *drawn*. Hermit gave the good Waler Ellerton 7 lbs. The Arab came out full of running, and won hands down, doing the 2 miles in 3 min. 51 secs.

Hermit received weight from Voltige, but it is possible he might have given her weight the following day; indeed, had different tactics been employed in the Trades Cup, had Hermit made the running instead of lying third, and running up to her twice, the results might have been different. At Burdwan, 1860, Hermit defeated the English horse Cockscomb (possibly by Chanticleer out of Yorkshire Lass). Many of these performances will show the capability of the Arab to carry weight and race. 3 miles, under 9 st. 5 lbs., in 5 min. 54 secs., is no mean performance.

The gray Arab Exile, carrying 11 st. 7 lbs., ran half a mile in 57 secs., and came home the next half-mile in a hand-gallop in 1 min. 3 secs., thus performing the mile in 2 min. with the greatest ease.

The gray Arab Salonica, carrying 10 st. 5 lbs., won a mile race easily in 1 min. 56 secs.

The Arab Elepoo, carrying 11 st. 7 lbs., ran the mile home for the Great Welter under 1 min. 58 secs., performing the whole distance, 1¾ mile and 15 yards, in

3 min. 34 secs.; and, carrying 10 st. 7 lbs., ran $1\frac{1}{2}$ mile in 2 min. 55 secs., winning in hand.

The bay Arab Glenmore, carrying 11 st., won the Winners' Handicap at Madras, in two heats; distance, $1\frac{3}{4}$ mile; the first heat in 3 min. $28\frac{1}{2}$ secs., the second in 3 min. 28 secs.

The true running and determination of the Arab are shown by the following account of the running of the gray Arab Crab, and the bay Arab Oranmore, at Calcutta, 1845. They met for the Bengal Cup (heats), 2 miles; they had previously run three or four well-contested races, winning alternately. For the Bengal Cup they ran five heats. The first won by Oranmore, second a dead heat, third won by Crab, fourth a dead heat, fifth heat won by Crab; weight 8 st. 7 lbs. each. These two horses met again the following month for a sweepstakes, round the course, $1\frac{3}{4}$ mile and 15 yards. A splendid rush on the part of each ended in a dead heat; time 3 min. 27 secs. Deciding heat won by a head by Oranmore; time 3 min. 25 secs. Crab carried 9 st., Oranmore 8 st. 12 lbs. Surely this is something like the stuff of which race horses should be made! The above-mentioned statistics establish the following facts:—That the Arab, even as known in India, has speed. Secondly, that he can maintain his speed over a distance of ground. Thirdly, that size (or height rather) has really nothing to do with speed or stride. Some may be willing to admit the merits of the Arabian, but will say, we cannot allow the Arabian to be a racer if he does not possess so great a flash of speed as our present breed; nor attempt to use him as a sire unless he can show superior speed. Nor would the public submit to the spectacle of Arabians racing when they could witness an exhibition of greater speed by our own English horses.

Well, be that as it may; for my own part—and I trust I may not be alone—I would prefer seeing a field of honest, pure-bred, handsome horses like Honeysuckle and Selim running hardly-contested races of 2 and 3 miles than scurries over a T.Y.C. After having bred racers, and exclusively for speed, for many generations, have we arrived at a very great difference in speed? Does it compensate for the bottom, determination, and honesty which are wanting? Has it never struck breeders that the natural speed of the pure Arabian might have been increased to even a greater degree than that now exhibited by his half-bred descendant, the English thorough-bred horse, if Arabian blood had been bred from alone for only a few generations, and that his other good qualities and characteristics might have been retained? Besides, is not the public often treated to the spectacle of witnessing races run in worse time than that made by Arabs? The pleasure of seeing a field of really beautiful horses honestly contesting for a prize is worth looking at.

But has it been proved yet that Arabians have not as high a rate of speed? Have we gone to Arabia and procured young stock, and by careful training ascertained their capabilities in that respect? Have we taken the pains to procure choice mares in foal, so that their produce might be born and reared in this country, developed, trained, and tried? Have we tried the plan of breeding horses of pure Arabian blood, and trying the young stock in the first, second, and third generation? Until all this has been tried and proved, who can say that the Arabian is inferior in speed to the English racer? It is only an unfounded assertion. Has any trouble been taken at all about the matter? The answers are simply in the negative.

Formerly the training of Arabs consisted in galloping a good honest game horse so many times round a race course. A somewhat improved system, since 1838, has shown that from such Arabs as go to India the time has improved from 2 miles in 4 min. to 2 miles in 3 min. 48 secs., and from 3 miles in 6 min. or 6 min. 7 secs. to 3 miles in 5 min. 54 secs., but the improvement is not necessarily limited to this; but with such natural speed to start upon, if these horses were bred from exclusively, in a few generations what might we not hope for!

Much as the Arab has been appreciated in India, little or no trouble has been taken to secure the importation of first-class Arabs; and even there, comparatively few really know an Arab horse.

The love of size which Englishmen have, has been for a long period detrimental to the importation of good Arabians into India. Size was demanded. The Arab merchant would plead in vain that it was no real criterion. Eventually the gentleman from England with European taste would find some one less scrupulous to accommodate him, and horses not of quite pure blood on the dams' side would be imported to please him, and, except to the fastidious or initiated, as taking or even more so to the European eye. This, I feel sure, has been one of the reasons why more horses like Barefoot and Honeysuckle have not found their way there. The latter horse was disliked on his first appearance on account of his want of size, and called an impostor and a brute. But Sheik Ibraheen-bin-Alee, of Calcutta celebrity, quietly remarked, 'Very well, gentlemen, you will see *what* a horse he will prove!' and when, in the following season, 'the denounced' did prove a distinguished winner, added, 'Gentlemen, I told you so! You will never meet his like again!' His end was a sad one; he was burnt to death going up the Ganges in the steamer 'Benares.'

It is related that about the close of the last century, an Arab horse was taken to Madras, and 6,000*l.* demanded for him. 1,000*l.* was eventually offered; the offer was indignantly refused, and the horse taken back. I find, also, that in 1797 a horse of extraordinary merit was sent to Bombay, evidently in very poor condition, and out of all form, from neglect and bad usage, an Arab called King David, 14 hands 1½ inch high. He was entered to make up one for the Aged Plate of 800 rupees, at Bombay, with little hope of his saving his distance. He started with three others; he won the first heat with great ease, distancing two of his three competitors, and won the second very easily. The next month being February, 1798, he ran a match for 10,000 rupees (1,000*l.*), with a famous Arab horse called Antelope, which was brought down from Surat, it was supposed, on purpose to beat King David. Antelope was acknowledged to be the fleetest horse that was ever remembered at Surat by the oldest natives, and the gentlemen of that station positively asserted that on trial he ran a mile *within the minute.*[1] The race was run at score all round. King David took the lead at starting, and kept it, winning by about three lengths. It is stated, King David, changing hands at this time, improved very much in appearance. At the second Bombay Races, December, 1798, he again started for the Aged Plate against his former competitor Antelope and three others. Antelope was made favourite, his former defeat being attributed to his having been landed out of a boat, on his passage from Surat, the day before he ran. To the astonishment of all, King David won with the greatest ease, and it was generally supposed, had he been pushed, could have distanced the whole the first heat.

On January 14, 1799, at Madras, he won 100*l.* with great ease, and on the 19th another race. In 1800, at Bombay, he won three several matches, beating Brown Bess, Dragon, and the famous mare Arabella. He never carried *less* than 10 st. 3 lbs., and no horse would after that appear against him.[2]

[1] The author does not pretend to endorse this assertion; it is similar to the tradition of the English wonder, Flying Childers; but we may be well assured that, in both instances, such assertions were not made, nor could the tradition have originated, without the display of some extraordinary power and speed.

[2] It is probable, Arabella was the chestnut mare foaled in 1792 by Rockingham, her dam Rachel by Highflyer.

Here we have a horse worthy to be put in the same roll or category as Flying Childers, and the accounts of their performances are very similar.

Although numerous instances could be brought forward, sufficient have been given to prove that the Arabian is worthy to be considered as a race horse himself, and is pre-eminently suited to found a breed of thorough-bred racers.

It is often urged that Mr. Attwood[1] and General Angerstein tried the Arab *cross*, and it failed. I answer, they never tried breeding from Arabs on both sides and cultivating the pure breed.

The fact of the occasional produce of an Arab horse and an English thorough-bred mare being unsuccessful, by not showing the average speed of a racer, proves nothing. Have such mares produced racers to other sires? Some of those of the Angerstein cross have run respectably; some have been winners; and Fair Ellen, daughter of the Eastern horse called 'The Wellesley Grey Arabian,' was the dam of Lilias, winner of the Oaks in 1826, and of The Exquisite, who ran second for the Derby in 1872.

It has been suggested that, although the horse bred for racing in England may possess a higher rate of *speed* than the Arabian, yet that *the public may often witness races run by English horses in worse time than that made by Arab horses in running over like or similar distances.* The account of the running of some Arabs

[1] Several of Mr. Attwood's, which were never trained, turned out excellent hunters.

in India, which is given in a former part of this chapter, proves the suggestion to be fact; but to make it more apparent, and to save the trouble of reference, I give two tables, one showing the time occupied in running for the 'Epsom Derby,' during a period of fifteen years taken in succession, with the single exception of the race in 1861, Kettledrum's year, in which instance the horses were started some 50 yards in advance of the post (the time was the same in Blair Athol's year); the other giving the performances of certain Arabs before mentioned, in which account the accuracy of the distances, weights, and timing may be depended upon. I selected the Epsom Derby because the distance was exactly 1½ mile. It is the race of the year, contested by the 'crack' horses of the year, and perhaps the best criterion we have in England. The period includes the Flying Dutchman's and Blair Athol's years, the latter the fastest Derby on record.

Horses.	Distance.	Time.
The Flying Dutchman	1½ mile	3 min.
Voltigeur	,,	2 ,, 50 sec.
Teddington	,,	2 ,, 51 ,,
Daniel O'Rourke	,,	3 ,, 2 ,,
West Australian	,,	2 ,, 55½ ,,
Andover	,,	2 ,, 52 ,,
Wild Dayrell	,,	2 ,, 54 ,,
Ellington	,,	3 ,, 4 ,,
Blink Bonny	,,	2 ,, 45 ,,
Beadsman	,,	2 ,, 45 ,,
Musjid	,,	2 ,, 59 ,,
Thormanby	,,	2 ,, 55 ,,
Caractacus	,,	2 ,, 45½ ,,
Macaroni	,,	2 ,, 50½ ,,
Blair Athol	,,	2 ,, 43 ,,

The Arab Horse	Distance.	Time.	
The Child of the Isles . .	$1\frac{1}{2}$ mile	2 min. 48 sec.	(won in a canter)
The Arab horse Elepoo . .	$1\frac{3}{4}$,,	3 ,, 20 ,,	
Elepoo, carrying 10 st. 7 lbs.	$1\frac{1}{2}$,,	2 ,, 55 ,,	(winning easily)
The Arab Glenmore, carrying 11 st. . .	$1\frac{3}{4}$,,	3 ,, 28 ,,	
The Arab Oranmore, 2nd heat	$1\frac{3}{4}$ mile 15 yds.	3 ,, 25 ,,	

Or compare the Flying Dutchman, 5 years old, standing 15 hands 3 inches, carrying 8 st. $8\frac{1}{2}$ lbs., winning the 2-mile match at York in 3 min. 55 sec., with the performance of the Arab Honeysuckle, 5 years old, standing 14 hands 1 inch, carrying 8 st., winning his 2-mile race in 3 min. 48 sec.; and the old Arab hunter Selim, carrying 9 st. 5 lbs., winning his 3-mile race in 5 min. 54 sec. It is noteworthy that heavy weights seem to have very little influence upon the running of these Arabs.

These examples are not offered to prove the Arab as known in India a speedier racer than the best in England, but I maintain they do show him to be possessed of speed, courage, endurance, and to be essentially a weight-carrier, and worthy the name of a courser or racer. You cannot call a horse that can do his 2 miles in 3 min. 48 sec. or 3 miles in 5 min. 54 sec. a slow horse.

The Arab may not be so speedy as the racer bred exclusively for speed for the last half-century, yet it cannot be denied, the performances of Arabs compare very favourably with those of English racers.

An Arab has been brought from India, and very occasionally trained, most likely when he has lost his speed, and because such a horse has failed to be successful against a field of English racers, it is said the Arab is not a racer. A likely colt was bought a few years ago at the annual sale of yearlings at Middle Park, and taken to Australia—by Gladiateur—his dam a Stockwell mare. Every care was taken of him, he was trained and raced, and although I am assured he ran gamely on several occasions, he had not the speed to contend successfully with the Australians; he was invariably beaten: ergo, the English thorough-bred of the best blood is not a racer.

On the other hand, in March 1872, the Australian Cup, a sweepstakes of 20 sovs. with 300 sovs. added, 2¼ miles, was won after three heats by Saladin, a son of Pegasus, an imported Arab, beating a field of seven horses. Saladin, the half Arab, aged, carried 7 st. 8 lbs., and Flying Dutchman, 6 years, 7 st. 5 lbs., made a dead heat after a splendid finish. Time, 4 min. 12 secs. The dead heat was run off at 5 o'clock, and after a close run race, resulted in another dead heat. Time 4 min. 15 secs. At 6 o'clock they started again, when the half Arab Saladin proved the winner by a good neck. Time, 4 min. 15 secs.[1]

[1] Dagworth, at Sydney, won the Great Metropolitan Stakes, 2 miles. The hero of the meeting was the great-grandson of an Arab. Dagworth is by Yattendon, his dam Nutcut by Pitsford, grandam by Glaucus (an Arab).

CHAPTER II.

The Arab as a hunter and charger—Considered as a hunter—Jurham and the Forbes Cup—Considered as a war horse—Arab blood likely to give better horses for cavalry and artillery—The French in Africa—Performances of certain horses—Ninety-mile match across the Desert—Match in Madras—Certain essential constitutional points more likely to be transmitted to half-bred stock either as hunters or troop horses by the Arabian than the English horse—Dissertation on the chest and its functions—Proper form of chest : to be found in the Arabian horse—Remarks by Youatt—The different formation in the modern thoroughbred horse affects all other half-bred stock—The Arabian the founder of the best breeds in India.

WE will next proceed to consider how admirably the Arabian is adapted to improve the character of half-bred stock for purposes of field sports and for the army.

As a hunter and war-horse the Arabian has been celebrated from all time. As a hunter, from when, in early time, he was employed to ride down the ostrich and the wild ass in his native country, to the present day, when he carries the expatriated Englishman over the plains of Hindostan up to the haunches of the wild pig, faces the tiger, or, single-handed, gallops down the wild deer and antelope ; and, complying with the manners and customs of the age, becomes a steeplechaser and wins the Forbes Kadur Cup over a four-mile course, stated by an experienced steeplechase-rider to have been more difficult and severe than any country or course in England, which, in 1871, Jurham, the only Arab in the race, among a good field of horses, wins with ease, the Arabian has ever proved himself a horse of unmatched courage and endurance. The tall and heavy grass, said to be so difficult and exhausting for so *small* and light a horse to force his way through, and other difficulties in the course, proved to be rather destructive to the Arab's opponents, as Jurham had speed and bottom left in him, in the last half-mile of tolerably open ground, when called upon to shoot away from his horses and win easily.

The high courage, the suppleness, the spring and elasticity, the compact but developed form, and great muscular development of the Arabian must cause him to be the horse best adapted for a hunter.

These qualities render him also more desirable than any other horse as a sire for begetting half-bred stock, either for hunting or for the military service. A horse of pure blood is more likely to implant and stamp his own good points and qualities upon properly selected stock, and in a greater degree, than a horse of less pure blood, such as the so-called English thorough-bred horse; more especially, too, when the latter horse does not possess the combination of excellences of the former. In the hunting-field, whenever a horse has possessed any direct Arab blood, he has always shown himself an excellent and superior hunter. This was the opinion of no less a udge than Davis, the late Royal Huntsman.

As a war-horse, from the days when he carried his

relentless rider, as on a whirlwind, upon Job's possessions, when he carried conquests from his birthplace to the confines of China in the east and the Atlantic on the west, to the present time, when, in the East, he leads the charge of England's chivalry, he has ever shone pre-eminent.

In India, certainly the best field for our cavalry, as a charger the Arab has always maintained the highest position. The Arabian horse has done his share in the conquests of that country.

I am fully persuaded if horses for both cavalry and artillery were bred from suitable mares from Arab horses, a marked difference and superiority would be the result, and we might then truly boast of having the best cavalry in the world. The French had to discard the European horse when in Africa, and re-mount their cavalry on such horses of Arab blood as they could procure, and these carried a weight of twenty-five stone. General Daumas may well exclaim, 'Now, a horse that, in a country often rough and difficult, marches and gallops, ascends and descends, endures unparalleled privations, and goes through a campaign with spirit, with such a weight on his back, is he or is he not a war-horse?'

Are our cavalry so mounted? What is the opinion of the War Office? Is not the Arabian horse worthy of their consideration?

Abd-el-Kader has stated that an Arab horse can travel a distance of fifty English miles day after day, and this without fatigue, for three or four months; and if required could accomplish 150 miles in one day, but should be carefully ridden the next, and only go a much shorter distance. Two instances recorded by General Daumas are worthy of consideration. On one occasion a young Arab, Si-Ben-Zyon, rode his father's mare eighty French leagues within twenty-four hours. She was watered only once, and had but eaten some leaves from the dwarf-palm while her rider had lain down by her side to sleep; yet she was not done up, and, as Si-Ben Zyon said, was capable of still performing a further journey. The next: 'All the old officers' (says General Daumas) 'of the Oran Division can state how, in 1837, a general, attaching the greatest importance to the receipt of intelligence from Tlemcem, gave his own charger (an Arab horse) to an Arab to go to procure the news. The latter set out from Château Neuf at 4 a.m., and returned at the same hour on the following day, having travelled seventy leagues (French) over ground very different from the comparatively level desert.' This latter confirms the former, and is a very valuable instance, as the distance had been measured, and was well known, and is sufficient warranty to induce belief in the reported great capabilities of the Arabian, which are but too often, in this country, regarded as only tales of the East and Oriental exaggerations. Moreover, the Arabs are just and true in their accounts and descriptions, although couched in language full of imagery. But are not we ourselves a very boastful people, and very reluctant to admit excellence in others?

In the ninety-mile match between an English thorough-bred horse and an Arab across the desert to Cairo, a few years ago, the former broke down badly; the Arab came in alone, having accomplished the whole distance in 7 hours 52 minutes. There was but little difference in the weights at starting; they appear to have carried 10 st. 8lbs. and 10 st. respectively. On returning to weigh the rider of the Arab was some 5 lbs. under weight, and it is quite possible, had the rider of the English horse also weighed, it might have been found he had lost as much weight.

At Madras a match was made by an officer of Horse Artillery and some officers of the 15th Hussars (then disbelievers in the Arabian); the former was to ride his Arab horse, about 14 hands 1 inch, 400 miles in five days. The Arab won the match with ease, without distress, and was none the worse after the performance, and his owner offered to do it again after resting one day.

The peculiar and perfect development of the Arabian (I say peculiar, as the same is not found in any other breed)—I now allude more especially to the chest, which has been noticed in a former part of this work, and which is one of the great secrets of the Arabian's endurance—is more likely to be transmitted to half-bred stock, either as hunters or for troopers—for both equally essential—by a horse who has this formation as a distinguishing point of his race or breed, than by a horse who may fail in this respect, or whose class or breed only possesses it in a modified degree, and which has been derived in the first place from the Arabian. Too round and too heavy a chest, however good it may be for heavy draught and slow work, is not adapted to rapid and continuous progression. Horses possessing narrow chests and flat sides are often spirited, very fast, but are incapable of continued work. Neither of this kind are suitable to the hunter or trooper, nor fit to be the sire of horses for such purposes. Although the latter, being often a horse of high speed, may be successful in half-mile races, he ought not to be considered a race horse. To fully explain the advantages of the Arabian as a sire, the use of the chest should be considered. Youatt says, 'The contents of the chest are the lungs and the heart: the first to render the blood nutrient and stimulating, and to give or restore to it that vitality which will enable it to support every part of the frame in the discharge of its function, and devoid of which the complicated and beautiful machine is inert and dead; and the second, to convey this purified arterialized blood to every part of the frame.'

'In order to produce and to convey to the various parts a sufficient quantity of blood, these organs must be large. If it amounts not to hypertrophy, the larger the heart and lungs the more rapid the process of nutrition, and the more perfect the discharge of every animal function.' He then explains the circular chest is clearly not advantageous, for it cannot expand, but every change of form would be a diminution of capacity, whereas the contents of the chest are 'alternately expanding and contracting.'

After instancing the description of chest found in cobs and some of our saddle-horses as being round enough, and therefore valued, as they seldom lose their condition, or tire if allowed to go their own pace—and that not altogether a slow one—Youatt observes very truly, if examined the chest will be found to be between the circle and ellipse, thus allowing of expansion, while retaining capacity. He next proceeds to describe the chest more particularly adapted to rapid progression combined with strength. *The broad deep chest* possessing 'considerable capacity in a quiescent state, and the power of increasing that capacity when the animal requires it'—this is the chest required by the race-horse, the hunter, and the cavalry horse.

'There must be,' says Youatt, 'the broad chest for the production of muscles and sinews, and the deep chest, to give capacity or power of furnishing arterial blood equal to the most rapid exhaustion of vitality.' 'This form of chest,' he further states, 'is consistent with lightness, or at least with all the lightness that can be rationally required. The broad-chested horse, or he that, with moderate depth at the girth, swells and barrels out immediately behind the elbow, may have as light a fore-hand and as elevated a wither as the horse with the narrowest chest; but the animal with the barrel approaching too near to rotundity is invariably heavy about the shoulders, and low in the shoulders.' Although this is sufficiently plain to all who thoroughly know the horse, it may require a little explanation to others who may not be so well initiated. The *round* chest is accompanied with a heavy shoulder, and is only applicable to draught; that it is not sufficient for a horse to have a very *deep* chest at the girth—seen sometimes to an exaggerated extent or to a fault—if that chest is narrow and flat. A horse of such formation might have great speed, but would not be capable of prolonged or continued exertion. A *chest* '*of moderate depth at the girth*' (often looking not so deep as it really is), but which '*swells and barrels out immediately behind the arms*,' is the one for insuring combined speed and bottom. Youatt next states how such a formation has been obtained, and may be obtained—namely, from the Arabian horse. 'It is to the mixture of Arabian blood that we principally owe this peculiar and advantageous formation of the chest of the horse.' Such a chest is compatible with the lightest shoulders. For the Arabian has the *lightest* shoulders—*lighter* than, but not so thin as is seen in any other breed or kind of horse. 'The Arab is light, *some* would say too much so before, but immediately behind the arms the barrel almost invariably swells out, and leaves plenty of room, and *where it is most wanted* for the play *of the lungs, and at the same time where the weight does not press so exclusively on the fore legs, and expose the legs to injury*.'

A contrary kind of chest being the type generally seen in the modern thorough-bred horse, a deep but narrow chest, reveals the secret of half-mile or short races having become so general, and marks him as not so fitting or capable of begetting weight-carrying and enduring hunters and hardy, serviceable troop-horses, capable of long-continued exertion, and occasionally great speed, as the Arabian horse, who possesses this form of chest in the highest perfection. This most important point in the form of a horse is further commented upon by the same author: 'An elevated wither or oblique shoulder, or powerful quarter, are great advantages; but that which is most of all connected with the general health of the animal, and with combined fleetness or bottom, is a deep and broad and swelling chest.'

If artificial breeds of horses are required for hunting and the army in this country, why refuse to use the Arabian as a sire, seeing that this essential conformation is one of his attributes, and only possessed by other breeds formerly improved by him in a modified degree? Of all horses in the world the Arabian possesses the deepest chest; but this is often overlooked or unobserved, for it is not so apparent at a casual glance, owing to the swelling barrel and long back ribs, which of course take off from the appearance of depth. Now, in a flat-sided horse, what depth there may be is at once seen, and appears often exaggerated, from the lightness of the hinder ribs. Deterioration is said to have taken place, and short races are in vogue. In conformation the modern horse appears deep enough in chest, but flat-sided. From the portraits of old racers (mostly badly executed) we see less apparent depth at the girth, but a more swelling barrel and deeper back ribs, the line of belly being far straighter. These horses ran over long courses; it was the fashion in those days. Perhaps the fashion was guided by the constitution and capabilities of the horse.

This formation in the so-called thorough-bred horse does and must necessarily affect all other breeds in the country; the standard or chief breed gives the tone to all others—to our hunters and troop-horses.

Colonel Shakespeare states, the horses in the Hyderabad Deccan are superior to any other native breed in India. They owe their superiority to the pure stock from which they were derived, the Arabian. So many as 500 Arab horses were imported into the Deccan at the commencement of this century. The best troop-horses bred in the late Company's studs had Arab horses for their sires. The most successful Government stud was one in the Madras Presidency, and that was because the high-caste Arab was almost entirely used as a sire.

The horses of the Hyderabad Deccan possess many of the fine points and qualities of their progenitors, the Arabians. Their temper, endurance, freedom from disease, longevity, capability of work and keeping condition on small quantities of food, their high courage and natural aptitude for being broken in, together with their attachment to their riders, come direct from the desert blood. Such qualities are admirable for all descriptions of riding-horses, and especially for cavalry horses, and, it would appear, can only be obtained by direct Arab blood.

During the late war it was constantly reported from many sources that horses derived partly from Arabian blood stood the hardships of a European campaign much better than all others; and in a letter which appeared in 'The Times,' February 24, 1871, giving an account of the entrance of Bourbaki's army into Berne, and the distressing appearance of the men, it was stated: 'The horses present a still worse appearance, seeming more fitted for the knacker's yard than to bear their burdens, although *undoubtedly* the Arabs justify the established reputation of their breed for endurance by the very tolerable condition they present, and the comparative *elasticity* of their paces.'

Although other Governments may be drawing large supplies from this country, and may be well-advised in so doing, it is no proof that they would not do better in procuring purer blood, which they may be doing also; and certainly no excuse for us to remain satisfied with an imperfect breed, when we might easily obtain a better.

The head of a horse is the index to his character, moral and physical. A breeder who was lamenting some coarseness or deficiency in the head of a colt of which he had expected great things, in reply to the consolation a friend was offering by pointing out the colt's otherwise almost perfect form, remarked: 'Never mind the rest of his body, if the head had only been all right, the body would have grown to it, but now his body can never get beyond his head.' This is too often overlooked in this country; indeed, it would appear, the head, the index, is little thought of; but it will, perhaps, explain why so many animals, apparently of early promise, never improve or show to advantage at maturity. A small head is not necessarily a beautiful or good head, although smallness is very often among horses of even racing blood the only recommendation, for the head may still be vulgar in appearance and very deficient.

Now, certainly, there is no head like the Arabian's. It is the true index to his character and form. Thus writes a member of the Veterinary profession. 'Fire and sagacity, blood and action, speed and bottom, are all the *natural attributes* of a horse having such a head.' But the Arabian horse alone possesses it. The Arabian's is not altogether a small head, it is, on the contrary, large in all parts containing the working and essential organs, it is small in those parts only which connect these essential organs. The same professional man says 'that which is set down as the handsomest of heads, turns out to be, on examination, the most serviceable.' Such being the case with the head of the Arabian, the index, so is it also with the rest of his body, every part is in harmony and proportion ; he is a large horse in every essential point and part of action and motion ; as no other horse has such a head, so no other horse possesses so fine and perfect a form. The Arabian is identical with utility. In this is his rare beauty.

What we call the thorough-bred horse, in spite of the great esteem in which he is held, cannot be called the saddle horse of the country. How few ever ride one. Look through a stud of hunters, how rarely a thorough-bred horse is seen. Is an entire stud of thorough-bred hunters to be met with? Comparatively speaking, how seldom he is found as a hack or riding horse. He is seldom seen as a cavalry charger, and he has not been successful in producing good troopers for our cavalry in India.

Yet the racer ought to be essentially a saddle horse. We ought not to have to raise a class of horses for the saddle, exclusive of the thorough-bred horse. The Arabian is a racer, a war horse, and hunter, a riding horse par excellence.

CONCLUSION.

It is evident the original framers of the Stud Book looked upon the Eastern horse, and *par excellence* the Arabian, as the pure-bred or thorough-bred horse, and among our horses those alone who are descended from Eastern horses, and are registered in the Book, are now considered thorough-bred, an acknowledgment of the superiority of Arabian blood. But another great boon is conferred by the Stud Book. It shows us most conclusively that our horse is not entirely of Eastern, still less of Arabian blood, and, in fact, is not really thorough or true bred. The character of our horse ebbs and flows, rises to comparative excellence, or sinks into mediocrity, as choice, or fashion, or the taste of the breeder may hit upon a selection in sire or dam possessing a larger or less amount of Arabian blood ; but it cannot get beyond a certain point of excellence ; it is impossible of permanent improvement. The mixed blood from which our horse has sprung will ever prevent him from attaining a permanent standard of excellence. The same cause must always have a tendency to degeneration, even if that should not have taken place—which many good authorities pronounce to be the case—and his altered form and want of stoutness would warrant that assertion. Seeing, then, that pure blood is essential for the establishment of a thorough good breed of horses, that our own is imperfect and deficient in blood, the only true way of meeting the difficulty, the only effectual one, the least expensive, and the quickest, is to start afresh with pure Arabian blood. Starting from a sure foundation (purity of blood), we have only to educate and develope excellences. There is no doubt horses of pure Arabian blood, bred in this country, would attain to a larger size; and there is every reason to believe the increase would be in due proportion, thereby insuring with the size increase of speed and strength. The increase of size or height obtained by our present thorough-bred horse has not been in proportion; it has led to many exaggerations. The increase of height from 14½ hands to 16 hands has been accomplished by greater length of limb. This, again, as a rule, has been owing to a greater length of cannon bone, without a corresponding length of radius or arm. Here is a great mechanical disadvantage. We will suppose two horses of equal height and power; the moral qualities, such as temper, courage, and nervous energy, also equal; but one shall be an inch longer in the cannon bone than the other, although the relative length of the fore legs shall be the same. The horse with the shorter cannon bone, and therefore longer radius, must, of necessity, be a speedier horse, and not only speedier, but, because the one has a great mechanical advantage, he would be a more lasting horse. Increase of height thus obtained may have been one of the causes of an increase of speed in the English racer over the Arab, but it tells against him over long courses and constant work, which brings him back again below the level of the Arabian. But if we establish a breed of pure Arabians, in which we have increased the size to 15 hands 2 inches, we have every reason to believe, with only proper care and treatment, the perfect form of the original will be retained; we may reasonably expect equal speed to the modern racer, if not greater, but accompanied with lasting qualities and endurance. The course to pursue is the attainment of a certain number of pure-bred Arabian horses and mares: the latter would most likely be in foal. It would be better if the Government would undertake this, and, indeed, engage to form such a national stud, as it could then be carried on in its integrity, without let or hindrance from the whims or fancies of private individuals.

A few well-selected persons, with knowledge of the Arabian horse and where to seek for him, would be the first thing needful. Should the Government not feel able to undertake it as a national scheme, there is a grand opening for private enterprise, or for a combination of gentlemen who have the welfare of the horse at heart. (It does not seem more unreasonable that there should be a stud for the production of horses entirely of pure or Arabian blood, than that companies should be formed for the breeding of racing stock of inferior and mixed blood.) In this the Government might help by granting certain plates or purses to be run for by Arabians and by their pure descendants. While the Middle Park Stud was intact, I abstained from giving the opinion of the late lamented proprietor, when this Arab scheme was brought to his notice, a few years ago. Mr. Blenkiron acknowledged the correctness of the theory. He said, 'It certainly would have been the only true plan upon which to have started; I can see that plainly. I tell you what; if it had been brought to my notice when I first commenced breeding, I would have done it; notwithstanding I have established my stud and have so much invested in it, were I only a few years younger, I would take it up myself now, and begin breeding again.' To be done at all it must be done well and thoroughly. It would be a great national benefit, for the prosperity of the horse is intimately connected with the welfare of a country:

> Effodere loco signum, quod regia Juno
> Monstrârat, caput acris equi: sic nam fore bello
> Egregiam et facilem victu per sæcula gentem.
>
> ÆNEIDOS, *lib. 1.*

'Afterwards Queen of cities, mistress of the seas, Carthage forgot the sign of what was to be her strength, became enslaved by commerce, and fell.'

The English horse is a compound of those found in Britain in Cæsar's time (whether introduced by the Kelt or Belgæ) the Roman horse—also a compound animal, or rather, many compound animals; then the Saxon horse, not unlikely of Persian extraction—even, perhaps, after the Persian had been improved by Arabian blood, but, in all probability, much modified and considerably changed during the progress of the Saxons from the Araxis to Jutland, and their long residence between the

Elbe and the Eider; then the Spanish horse, followed by that of Flanders; and upon this heterogeneous mass was engrafted Eastern and Arabian blood.

Can we wonder, then, at the want of harmony of parts and proportion in the animal, and the great diversity of types to be seen in that select class called thorough-bred (the present standard breed of the country)? I do not deny great merit in individual animals of mixed blood, but it is not possessed collectively, nor can animals of mixed blood keep up excellences.

But the advantages of pure blood are the maintenance and continuance of certain original good qualities and attributes, both moral and physical; and by establishing pure Arab blood in this country, with proper care we may expect to attain a degree of excellence hitherto unknown.

Many think the English horse is more nearly allied to the Barb than to the Arabian, and is more like the former in appearance and character, and argue that for any improvement the Barb should be selected. Beware of doing this. Seek always the pure and parent breed. That the English horse should have a closer resemblance to the Barb and to other Eastern horses, does not show that he has been derived more from such sources; but it is the natural consequence of his being of mixed blood, and only partly Arabian, and therefore very similarly bred to the Barb, Persian, and Toorkoman horse. The English horse being of a mixed breed cannot have the perfect form and character of the Arabian, therefore has gradually assumed the appearance of those breeds which have also been derived or improved by the Arabian, but whatever advantage it may be supposed he has drawn from the Barb and other horses of Eastern blood, has really been derived from the Arabian, who gave the excellence to those breeds.

'The Toorkomans trace their breed of horses to Arabian sires,' and procure Arab blood to invigorate their breed as often as opportunity may occur. The Persian is certainly a breed improved by the Arabian. It is stated that those horses bred in Kurdistan are accounted the best in beauty and strength—very likely they have received a further infusion of Arabian blood since the Shammar have occupied Mesopotamia. The Barb is a descendant of the Arabian, but certainly not always of pure blood.

A national stud is wanted. There is a cry for a system that shall supply good and useful horses. But some will say it must be for the production of good, sound, weight-carrying hunters; others want good riding horses for general purposes; the Government, horses for the army; the sportsman a racer. When, after the lapse of more than a century, our thorough-bred horse has failed to become our saddle horse, our hunter, does not supply our cavalry with hardy and useful horses, now is the time no longer to postpone the selection of the Arabian. The horse who in himself answers all these requirements, whose natural attributes are fire and sagacity, blood and action, speed and bottom.

The sportsman who loves racing for the sport itself may yet carry off the Blue Riband of the Turf with a horse of pure Arabian blood, and know he is conferring a lasting benefit on his country. The Welter weight might find himself carried in the first flight by a real weight-carrier of pure blood. The cavalry officer would have a charger worthy to carry him in front of his squadrons. All who are interested in riding would be benefited, for we should have a pure breed of *saddle-*horses.

Remarks on the future treatment of the Arabian horse in this country, to ensure the successful establishment of a new and pure breed, come not within the province of this work—the chief object of which is to point out that our thorough-bred horse is not pure; that a pure breed of horses does exist, and where it is to be found.

First let us obtain the pure bred and perfect horse, then let us take care to keep his future generations pure.

LIST

OF

ARABIANS, BARBS, TURKS, AND FOREIGN HORSES,

WHICH WERE EMPLOYED, MORE OR LESS,

IN THE FORMATION OF THE ENGLISH STUD,

FROM THE TIME OF KING JAMES I. UNTIL ABOUT THE END OF THE LAST CENTURY.

ARABIANS.

Markham's Arabian. A bay horse, bought by King James I.
Wilkinson's Bay Arabian, about 1680. King Charles II.'s reign.
An Arabian (sire of Bald Peg, Spanker's grandam).
Curwen's Chestnut Arabian, about 1700–1709.
The Leedes Arabian.
The Darley Arabian. A Bedouin Horse, of the family called Keheilan-Ras-el-Fedawi, imported by Mr. Darley the latter end of Queen Anne's reign.
The Basset Arabian, about 1700.
Harpur's Arabian, about 1700.
Pulleine's Chestnut Arabian, about 1700.
D'Arcy's Chestnut Arabian, about 1700–1710.
Hutton's Arabian, about 1700.
Cyprus Arabian, about 1715–1720.
Bloody Buttocks, a grey Arabian of Mr. Croft's, with a red mark on his hip.
Lord Lonsdale's Bay and Grey Arabians, about 1720.
Bethell's Arabian, about 1710–40 (sire of Salome, dam of Cypron, and grandam of King Herod).
Alcock's Arabian, about 1720.
Sir M. Newton's Arabian, about 1720–1745.
The Oglethorpe Arabian.
Lord Northumberland's Golden Arabian, about 1740–1760.
Duke of Northumberland's Chestnut, Bay, and Grey Arabians, about 1760–1780.
The Northumberland Brown Arabian (afterwards called Leedes Arabian), about 1760.
The Cullen Arabian, about 1740–1755.
The Coomb Arabian, about 1755–1780 (sometimes called the Pigot Arabian, and sometimes the Bolingbroke Grey Arabian).
His Majesty's one-eyed Grey Arabian (George I. or II.), about 1720–30.
Hampton Court Arabian, 1720.
Chestnut Litton Arabian, 1720
Oxford Bloody-shouldered-Arabian, 1700–22.
Oxford Arabian.

Oxford Dun Arabian (?).
Duke of Beaufort's White and Grey Arabians, 1720-40.
Conyers' Arabian, about 1730-40
Grosvenor Arabian, about 1750-70.
Saanah Arabian, 1760-80.
Stanyan's Arabian, about 1720-30.
Devonshire Arabian, Chestnut, about 1740-60.
Bell's Arabian, about 1760-72.
Blair's Arabian.
Bunbury Arabian, about 1760.
Widdrington Arabian, about 1710-1730.
Wynn Arabian, about 1710-30.
Ossory Arabian, about 1760-74.
Bright's Arabian, about 1730-46.
Newcomb's Arabian, about 1745-1758.
Lord Brook's Arabian, about 1720.
Mr. Fletcher's Arabian, about 1730-45.
Somerset Arabian, about 1725-40.
Panton's Arabian, 1750-62.
Milward's Arabian, about 1755-75.
Mr. Parker's Arabian, about 1770-80.
Damascus Arabian, about 1750-75.
Witham Grey Arabian, about 1760-76.
Wilson's Arabian, about 1740-60.
Ward's Arabian, about 1760-70.
Blackett's Arabian, about 1710-30.
Mr. Gibson's Arabian, about 1750-1770.
Clifton Arabian, about 1730-40.
Lord Rockingham's Arabian.
Sir John Sebright's Arabian.
Thompson's Grey Arabian.
Philippo's Arabian, about 1770-90.
General Evans's Arabian, about 1730.
General Smith's Arabian, 1760-77.
Woburn Arabian, 1780-1800.
Sir J. Jenkins' Arabian, about 1700-20.
Sir T. Gresley's Arabian, about 1700.
Sir R. Sutton's Grey Arabian, about 1730.
Sir W. Morgan's Arabian, about 1720.
Arcot Arabian, 1790.
Jilfy Arabian, 1760-70.
Bistern Arabian.
Pembroke Arabian.
Portland Arabian, about 1720.
Chesterfield Arabian.
Lord Cassilis' Arabian, about 1760-70.
Lord Heathfield's Arabian.
Lord Mansfield's Arabian.
Lord Winchilsea's Arabian.
Gregory's Arabian, about 1760-80.
Hall's Arabian, about 1710-20.
Ferrers' Arabian, 1760-76.
Ratcliff Arabian, about 1760.
Khalan Arabian, about 1750-70.
Clements' Arabian, 1770.
Richards' Arabian, about 1710-20.
Johnson's Arabian.
Storey's Arabian.
Morton Arabian.
Patnull Arabian.
Rumbold Arabian, 1787.
Barington Arabian.
Lexington Arabian, 1720.
Mr. Burlston's Arabian, 1750-70.
Williams' Woodstock Arabian.
Sir John Sebright's Arabian, 1740.
Thompson's Arabian, 1760-72.
Vernon Arabian, 1760.
Lord Finch's Arabian (afterwards Duke of Devonshire's, sire of Fair Wanderer), about 1730.
Lord Algernon Percy's Grey Arabian, about 1770-85.
Lord Bolingbroke's Arabian, 1760-80.
Ancaster Arabian, 1760.
Pembroke Arabian, 1780.

BARBS.

Dodsworth, foaled in England, was a natural Barb; his dam, a Barb mare, was imported in the time of King Charles II.

Greyhound, foaled in England in King William III.'s reign, was a natural Barb; his sire the White Barb Chillaby, his dam Slugey, a natural Barb mare.

Curwen's Bay Barb, was a present from the Emperor of Morocco to Lewis XIV. of France, brought into England by Mr. Curwen.
The Thoulouse Barb. Brought from France by Mr. Curwen; afterwards the property of Sir J. Parsons.
Croft's Bay Barb, was a son of Chillaby and the Moonah Barb Mare.
The Godolphin Barb, sometimes called an Arabian.
The Compton Barb, often called the Sedley Arabian.
Lord Fairfax's Morocco Barb, sire of Spanker's dam.
Taffolet Barb.
Chillaby Barb, white.
Chillaby Barb, black.
Wolseley Barb.
Hutton's Grey Barb.
,, Bay Barb.
Black Barb, without a tongue (King William III.'s)
Layton Barb.
Burton Barb.
White-legged Lowther Barb.
Panton's Grey Barb.
Sir H. Harpur's Barb.
Cole's Barb.
Lowther's Bay Barb.
Fenwick's Barb.
Vernon Barb.
Dun Barb.
Sir W. Morgan's Grey Barb,
,, ,, Black Barb.
Shafto's Barb.
Curzon's Grey Barb.
Lord Marsh's Barb.
Pelham's Barb.
Duke of Marlborough's little Mountain Barb.
Orford Barb.
Lord Townshend's Brown Barb.
Meadows' Barb.
Godolphin Grey Barb.
Massey's Grey Barb.
Wilkinson's Barb.
Lord Townshend's Barb.
St. Victor's Barb.
Cripple Barb.
Sir R. Mostyn's Bay Barb.
Sir J. Pennington's Barb.
Duke of Rutland's Black Barb.
Rider's Chestnut Barb.

TURKS.

The Hemsley Turk (Duke of Buckingham's).
Place's White Turk. (Mr. Place was Stud-master to Oliver Cromwell).
The Stradling, or Lister Turk. Brought into England from the siege of Buda, in the reign of James II.
The Byerly Turk. Capt. Byerly's charger, in King William's reign, 1689.
The D'Arcy White Turk.
The D'Arcy Yellow Turk.
The Selaby Turk. The property of Mr. Marshall, Stud-master to King William, Queen Anne, and King George I.
Sir J. Williams' Turk. (Also called the Honeywood Arabian.)
The Belgrade Turk. Taken at the siege of Belgrade by General Merci; afterwards purchased by Sir Marmaduke Wyvill; he died about 1740.
Phillips' Brown Turk, about 1740.
Orford Turk.
Stamford Turk.
Captain Rouksby's Turk.
Akaster Turk.
Westall Turk.
Mulso Turk.
Wilkinson's Turk.
Holderness Turk.
Ely Turk.
Bay Pigot Turk.
Lambert Turk.
Shaftesbury Turk.
Sir E. Hale's Turk.
Lord Hillsborough's Turk.
Sutton Turk.
Lord Carlisle's Turk.
Rutland Turk.
Paget Turk.

PERSIAN HORSES.

A Persian Stallion, the sire of the Duke of Rutland's Bonny Black's dam, foaled 1765.
Thompson's Persian, 1769.
Lord Burlington's Persian, 1752.
Commodore Mathews' Persian, 1729.
Mr. Howe's Persian, 1729

EGYPTIAN.

Mr. Croft's Egyptian.

FOREIGN HORSES.

Sir T. Gascoigne's.
A Foreign Horse in Diamond's pedigree.
Sir W. Goring's Foreign Horse.

ARABIAN MARES,

Which were employed in the formation of the English stud during the last century.

1. A Natural Arabian Mare, great-grandam of Mr. Bertie's Trifle, by Fox.

This mare in another place, p. 183, vol. i., 'General Stud-book' is called a Natural *Barb* Mare, an instance showing how horses of Eastern blood were not always accurately described, and that there was formerly, as there is now, a propensity to call any horse of Eastern blood an Arab. An inborn acknowledgment of the superiority and antiquity of the Arabian breed : no one possessing a pure Arabian would call him a Turk or Barb, or care to have him so described.

2. A Natural Arabian Mare, grandam of Lord Portman's Tiney, by Skim.
3. An Arabian Mare, great-grandam of Lord Lonsdale's Monkey, by his Bay Arabian.
4. An Arabian Mare, great-great-grandam of Sir C. Sedley's Cadena, by Cade.
5. An Arabian Mare of Lord Lonsdale's, great-great-grandam of Sir J. Pennyman's Bumper, by Partner.
6. An Arabian Mare, the dam of Sir C. Bunbury's Humdrum, by Matchem.
7. An Arabian Mare, the dam of Lord Clermont's Hunston.

There are two other Arabian Mares mentioned between the years 1760–80, but I am not sure if these were imported mares, or whether they were foaled in this country, and styled Arabian mares after their sires, as in the cases of the Beaufort, Cullen, the Cyprus, and the Darley Arabian Mares, which were daughters of those Arabians, and of mares more or less purely bred. The same may be the case with those mares numbered 3, 4, 5, 6, and 7. I do not say it is so ; they were in this country at an early date, but their description is certainly rather in opposition to those marked 1 and 2, which, being called Natural Arabian Mares, would imply they were imported, or, if foaled in this country, that their sires and dams were both Arabian.

BARB MARES.

1. A Barb Mare, grandam of Achilles, 1737.
2. A Natural Barb Mare, dam of Blossom.
3. The Moonah Barb Mare.
4. Layton Barb Mare.
5. A Barb Mare (the dam of Careless).
6. The Violet Layton Barb Mare.

7. Sir Hugh Cholmondeley's Barb Mare.
8. Barb Mare, great-grandam of Dyer's Dimple.
9. A Natural Barb Mare, great-grandam of Dismal, 1733.
10. The Burton Barb Mare.
10a. Mr. Burton's Natural Barb Mare.
11. Barb Mare, great-grandam of Grasshopper, 1731.
12. Barb Mare, dam of Grey Legs, 1725.
13. Barb Mare, dam of Look-about-you, 1734.
14. Natural Barb Mare, grandam of Old Smales.
15. The Barb Mare, great-grandam of Spanker.
16. A Barb Mare, dam of Dodsworth, imported in Charles II.'s reign, and called, a Royal Mare.
17. Slugey, a Natural Barb Mare, Greyhound's dam.
18. A Natural Barb Mare, great-great-grandam of The Darley Arabian Mare.
19. A Barb Mare, imported in 1750 by Admiral Keppel.
20. A Natural Barb Mare, great-grandam of a Childers' Mare.
21. Queen Anne's Moonah Barb Mare.
22. A Natural Barb Mare, great-great-grandam of Miss Layton (Lodge's Roan Mare). This Barb Mare was a present to Lord Arlington (Secretary of State to King Charles II.), from the Emperor of Morocco.
23. A Natural Barb Mare, great-grandam of Pintoes.
24. A Natural Barb Mare, great-grandam of a Whitefoot Mare.

PEDIGREES.

HORSES AND MARES OF EASTERN BLOOD.

BASTO — entirely of Eastern blood

- Byerly Turk
- Bay Peg
  - Leedes Arabian
  - Young Bald Peg
    - Leedes Arabian
    - Old Morocco Mare (Spanker's Dam)
      - Lord Fairfax's Morocco Barb
      - Old Bald Peg
        - An Arabian
        - a Barb Mare

Blossom a horse of Eastern blood

- Curwen's Bay Barb
- A Natural Barb Mare

---

descent

- Careless
  - Spanker
    - Yellow Turk
    - Daughter of
      - Morocco Barb
      - Bald Peg
        - An Arabian
        - a Barb Mare
  - Barb Mare
- Charming Jenny (Sister to Leedes)
  - Leedes Arabian
  - Daughter of
    - Spanker
      - Yellow Turk
      - Daughter of
        - Morocco Barb
        - Bald Peg
          - An Arabian
          - a Barb Mare
    - Daughter of (Spanker's Dam)
      - Morocco Barb
      - Bald Peg
        - An Arabian
        - a Barb Mare

Careless (Mr. Leedes') a horse entirely of Eastern blood

- Spanker
  - Yellow Turk (D'Arcy's)
  - Daughter of
    - Lord Fairfax's Morocco Barb
    - Bald Peg
      - An Arabian
      - a Barb Mare
- A Barb Mare

Bartlet's Childers

Supposed and generally acknowledged as own Brother to Flying Childers son of Darley Arabian and Betty Leedes

See Flying Childers' Pedigree

Lord Lonsdale's Counsellor a horse of Eastern descent

COUNSELLOR

- The Shaftesbury Turk
- Full Sister to Spanker
  - D'Arcy's Yellow Turk
  - Daughter of
    - Lord Fairfax's Morocco Barb
    - Bald Peg
      - An Arabian
      - a Barb Mare

Dyer's Dimple a horse of Eastern descent, bred by Mr. Leedes

DIMPLE

- Leedes Arabian
- Daughter of
  - Spanker
    - D'Arcy's Yellow Turk
    - Daughter of
      - Morocco Barb
      - Bald Peg
        - An Arabian
        - a Barb Mare
  - Daughter of
    - Dodsworth a Natural Barb foaled in England
    - a Barb Mare

DISMAL 1733
Lord Godolphin's Dismal a horse of Eastern descent

- Godolphin Arab or Barb
- Daughter of
  - Alcock's Arabian
  - Daughter of
    - Curwen's Bay Barb
    - a Natural Barb Mare

Highland Laddie (own brother to Leedes)
Highland Laddie (Lord D'Arcy's) a horse of Eastern blood

- Leedes Arabian
- Daughter of
  - Spanker (see his Pedigree)
  - Barb Mare (Spanker's Dam)
    - Morocco Barb
    - Bald Peg
      - An Arabian
      - a Barb Mare

LEEDES

- Leedes Arabian
- Daughter of
  - Spanker (see his Pedigree)
  - Daughter of (Spanker's Dam)
    - Lord Fairfax's Morocco Barb
    - Bald Peg
      - An Arabian
      - a Barb Mare

MONKEY 1725
Lord Lonsdale's Monkey a horse of Eastern descent

- Lord Lonsdale's Bay Arabian
- Daughter of
  - Curwen's Bay Barb
  - Daughter of
    - Byerly Turk
    - an Arabian Mare

Duke of Wharton's St. Martin a horse of Eastern blood — ST. MARTIN

- Spanker (a horse of Eastern blood)
  (See his Pedigree)
- Mr. Burton's Natural Barb Mare.

Mr. Pelham's Spanker a horse of Eastern descent — SPANKER

- D'Arcy's Yellow Turk
- Daughter of
  - Lord Fairfax's Morocco Barb
  - Bald Peg
    - An Arabian
    - a Barb Mare

Sir J. Parsons' Tifter

- Thoulouse Barb
- Sister to Leedes (a Mare of Eastern blood)
  (See Leedes' Pedigree)

Horse the son of

- Conyers' Arabian
- Daughter of
  - Dyer's Dimple (see his Pedigree)
  - Daughter of
    - King William's Black Bar[b]
    - Chillaby
    - Moonah Barb Mare

Arabian Mare, a Mare entirely of Eastern descent*

DARLEY ARABIAN MARE

Darley Arabian

Daughter of
- Byerly Turk
- Daughter of
  - Taffolet Barb
  - Daughter of
    - Place's White Turk
    - a Natural Barb Mare

* This mare was not put to an Arabian, nor to horses of Eastern blood, but only to Bay Bolton. She was the great-great-grandam of Woodpecker.

Mr. Wilkinson's Mare a Mare of Eastern blood*

Mr. Wilkinson's Bay Arabian

A Natural Barb Mare.

* This mare was the dam of the Duke of Wharton's Old Smales. Her dam, the Barb Mare, was bought by Mr. Wilkinson of Lord Arlington (Secretary of State to King Charles II.), to whom she was a present from the Emperor of Morocco.

LEEDES MARE

Leedes, a horse of Eastern descent. (See his Pedigree)

Moonah Barb Mare

LONDON: PRINTED BY
SPOTTISWOODE AND CO., NEW-STREET SQUARE
AND PARLIAMENT STREET